# Meditations for Transformation

Larry Moen

# NEW LEAF
*distributing company*

**Lithia Springs, Georgia**

Published by:        United States Publishing
                     Box 504
                     Captain Cook, HI 96704


Cover Art:           Charles Frizzell © "Ethereal Journey"


Illustrations:       Patty Smith


Printed in the United States of America.

Library of Congress Cataloging-in-Publication Data

Meditations for Transformation/ [edited by] Larry Moen
p.  cm.
Revised edition of: Guided imagery, v. 1.
ISBN 0-9627209-4-1
1. Meditation. 2. Imagery (Psychology) 3. Visualization.
4. Self-actualization (Psychology) I. Moen, Larry, 1948-
II. Guided imagery.
BF637.M4G85    1994
155.3'2 — dc20                                93-34925
                                                 CIP

To my sons and brothers Matthew and Lucas.

*Nothing surrounds everything,*
*Nothing is in everything,*
*Everything is Nothing.*

*– L.M.*

# Contents

**Healing** cont'd

**Relaxation & Stress Release**   85

**Freedom & Awareness**   119

# Introduction

At some point, we all seek to "transform" our lives. It may be a spiritual or physical transformation, the desire for a new career, or a change in relationship. Whatever the challenge of your transformation, this collection of guided meditations offers you many paths to facilitate that change, improve the quality of your life, move through your daily existence, and tap into your higher self.

The higher self consists of an inner core of pure beauty which is a descendant of Divine Energy. This beauty exists deep within and can be perceived as a hollow cylinder of vibration and light. The desire to see causes the reflection, and at that point loving light penetrates the perception of fearful darkness and transformation occurs, by turning inside out, or reversing.

Creative imagery is a tool that can change the inner knowledge and perceptions by allowing you to see the outside world from within first. Transformation occurs during the changing of the guard, or reality, from Nothing to Something or Something to Nothing.

*Meditations for Transformation* provides wonderful alternative realities from a cross-section of professionals including, physicians, psychologists, healers, teachers, and authors who have found ways to help themselves, and the people they love, attain inner change and growth.

I was first introduced to guided imagery at a workshop called "Healing Your Inner Child" taught by Margot Escott. My journey into healing and opening up to the love that is available to all of us inspired me to pursue many paths of personal growth, such as self-hypnosis, T'ai-Chi, yoga, visualization, chanting and other explorations. While experiencing these avenues, I found I was growing into a more calm, serene person.

In addition to its stress release benefits, guided meditation also is effective in treating stress related and physical illnesses, among them headaches, muscle spasms, and chronic pain. Many researchers have found that imagery is an important part of treatment programs for a variety of diseases. It has also been shown to improve memory.

Also, many athletes achieve peak performance in their particular sports through practicing meditative visualization. Professional golfers and tennis players are among those who use these techniques to improve their games. Visualizing that you can successfully manage a situation helps you confront and master that situation. Visualize yourself already accomplishing a goal, and your mind and body assume you have. Certain thoughts produce related emotions. If you think sad thoughts, you experience unhappiness. If you think fearful thoughts, you experience anxiety. If you think joyful thoughts, you experience happiness.

For example, think about your kitchen; close your eyes and imagine what the room looks like. Next, see if you can remember all the colors in your kitchen. Now imagine taking a piece of lemon, slicing it, putting it into your mouth, and taking a bite. Did you start to salivate? This is an example of intended thought into imagery. You now see that you do have the ability to change your reality.

When you enter this new reality family, you may discover your thoughts no longer control you, but that you are able to control your thoughts. The intent comes from center.

Just as a potter molds his clay, you are capable of transforming yourself in any manner you choose. You can change your programming. You can develop greater self-awareness and self-love and realize your full potential as a Spiritual Light Being having a human experience.

It is my hope that you will become the person you were truly meant to be. May you obtain inner peace, love, serenity, and happiness for the good you accomplish by guiding yourself and others. Good luck and happy images!

– L. M.
January 1994

# How To Use This Book

If you have never practiced guided imagery or meditation, do not be concerned. Everyone has visualized to some degree, and this book offers a variety of guided imageries that can be practiced by anyone following a few simple instructions. No special classes or courses are needed. If prayer is part of your life, then you have already experienced a kind of meditation. So relax and enjoy the journey.

## Types of Meditation

While traditional meditation requires a quiet unoccupied mind, guided imagery creates a scene or group of scenes developed to fulfill the purpose of the imagery. An imagery designed to help you get ahead in your career might involve climbing a mountain or finding your way on a difficult jungle path. The object of the journey is to help psychologically orient yourself for achievement, healing, relaxation, or numerous other areas of change or growth.

## Where and When Should I Meditate?

These journeys can be experienced by reading them silently or out loud alone or with a partner. You may wish to tape record journeys in your own voice and play them back at times best for you. You may also wish to share these journeys with a group.

Visualization can really be done anywhere. While waiting in a doctor's office, on an airplane, during a walk, or even sitting at your desk.

However, these journeys are best practiced in a quiet place where you will not be interrupted and where you can be in a relaxed position: with eyes closed lying down, sitting in a chair, or perhaps sitting in a cross-legged manner with your back straight. Do not choose a position because you think you should; choose the one most comfortable for you.

The best time for using a guided imagery is what is best for you. Often people will use uplifting, invigorating journeys to start their days; soothing, tension relieving imageries for midday breaks; and relaxing, creative visualizations for evenings.

Group meditations are useful for promoting creativity in work projects and for encouraging people to pull together for business or community activities. An excitable, rambunctious group of children can be calmed down using imagery as well.

## Pauses

Many journeys have one or more "pauses." The length of time you take at these pauses will depend on your own experiences: it can be a few minutes or an hour. You may determine the length of the pause before you begin or during the journey.

## What if I Fall Asleep?

Some people have such relaxing experiences that they believe they may have fallen asleep. Usually they have not. But to be sure, you can place one of your elbows in a upright position so that if you start to doze off, your arm will wake you up as it falls.

## Music

Music can enhance the journeys, providing it is quiet and does not contain abrupt changes in tempo or pitch. The tape "Creative Imagineering" is pure ambient music, which can develop or increase visualization abilities. An order form is located at the back of this book for this and other tapes.

## Breathing and Relaxation

All of the exercises contained in this book provide basic instructions for deep breathing at the beginning of each journey. Be aware that this breathing is not gasping or hyperventilation but deep, slow, controlled inhales and exhales. Most people breathe from their mid- or upper chests, but deep relaxing breath comes from "belly breathing." Inhale through your nose and expand your stomach. When you exhale, contract your stomach and gently force the air up through your lungs and out through your nose or mouth, whichever you prefer.

## But What if I Can't Visualize?

Give yourself permission to visualize. Allow your mind to play and create and expand on what images you do see. Be patient with yourself. Say to yourself "If I could visualize something what would it look like."

Begin by practicing with objects that are familiar to you. Imagine a room in your home, your favorite vacation spot, or the picture of a loved one. Add movement and color to the image and allow your mind to be free and wander through the pictures you are creating. Practice this as you would anything else and soon you will be able to visualize fantastic, imaginary scenes that will stimulate and enhance your guided journeys.

Turn now to journeys in this book. Look through them and choose the ones that are best for you at this time. You may wish to begin by reading them silently to yourself, then aloud.

Enjoy these journeys, their wonderful vivid images, their life-enhancing qualities, and their ability to help you achieve your goals and desires.

Transformation

# 1

# Creating the Silence

## Guide: John Bradshaw

*"In meditation, we simply let ourselves be."*

## Introduction

This meditation aims at enhancing your "beingness". When you are in touch with your beingness, you are one with everything that is. There is no longer any separation. Without separation there is no object or event outside of you to achieve....

In this meditation you can begin to experience pure moments of just being here. These moments feel open and spacious because they are devoid of personal needs, meanings and interpretations. This larger space is one way to describe the *silence*. Meditation can teach us how to contact this larger space or (silence). Since this space lies beyond the constant search for personal meaning, it can affect a radical transformation in the way we live. In shame-based lingo, this means you will give up your hypervigilance and guardedness. Meditation can lead you to this larger sense of aliveness. Such a sense of aliveness is not about anything we do; it's about who we are. As Jacquelyn Small says, "There is nothing that has to be done; there is only someone to be."

2

Creating the state of silence or mindlessness involves discipline. It is best compared to water dripping on a rock. Over the years the rock gets eaten away. The following is one of many ways the state of mindlessness can be approached.

## The Journey

Start by becoming aware of the sensation of air passing through your nostrils. Feel its touch. Notice in what part of the nostrils you feel the touch of the air when you inhale, and in what part of the nostrils you feel the touch of air when you exhale.... Become aware of the warmth or coldness of the air.... Breathe into your forehead and become aware of any sensations in your forehead....

Continue to be aware of any sensation around your eyes, around your mouth,... in your neck and shoulders.... Just be aware of the sensation.... Continue through your whole body. Omit no part of you.... You may find some parts of you completely devoid of sensation.... Keep focused on those parts. If no sensation emerges, move on....

Once you get to your toes, start over again.... Do this for about 10 minutes.... Then become aware of your body as a whole. Feel the whole of your body as one mass of various types of sensations.... Now return to the parts — focusing on your eyes, mouth, neck, etc..... Then once again rest in the awareness of your body as a whole.

Notice now the deep stillness that has come over you.... Notice the deep stillness of your body.... Go back to a part and come back to the stillness....

Try not to move any part of your body.... Each time you feel an urge, don't give in to it, just be aware of it as sharply as you can. This may be extremely painful for you at first. You may become tense. Just be aware of the tenseness.... Stay with it and the tension will disappear.

### Pause

Now imagine you are entering a holy place.... Walk toward a circular altar with a dirt floor.... There is a book buried in the dirt and you know where it is.... Dig it up and start looking through it until you find a page that draws you to it.... You may see a symbol on this page.... You may have a strong feeling about something you see... or you may read something that engages you.... Take whatever comes to you and return the book to the place you found it.... Walk out of the holy place and see yourself as you come out.... See the symbol or feeling or message you got from the book as if it were on a screen.... If what you experienced was a feeling, imagine that feeling taking some form. See yourself interacting with your symbol, feeling or message.

### Pause

Then let the whole horizon become darker and darker until there is nothing but darkness.... Gaze into the darkness.

### Pause

Begin to see a candle flame in the center of the darkness.... See the light from the flame growing brighter and brighter until the whole landscape is illuminated.... Gaze into a field of pure white light; let yourself be absorbed by the light.... Let yourself flow into the light.... Be aware of nothing. There is nothing, only a great abyss and emptiness.... Flow into the "nothingness."

## Pause

Slowly begin to see the number one on the horizon; then the number two. Very slowly see the number three, number four, five, six; when you see the number seven, open your eyes. Sit in reverie for a few minutes.

To be "mindless" is to be free of any mental content. In the silence, you stop all the inner voices. You turn off your mental chatter. The mind is emptied and focused on nothing (no-thing). Such a state is a state of pure being. Being is the ground of all the beings that are. There are human beings, animal beings, tree beings. Each is a specific form of being. Each is a thing. When the mind reaches a state of nothingness, it goes beyond all things to the ground of all things. When you get beyond anything you arrive at a place beyond any form of being. You arrive at pure being. So to get to the nothingness, you actually get to the ground of everything. You become united to being itself. In such a state you are connected to everything.

*John Bradshaw, author of best-selling* Bradshaw On: The Family *and television host for the PBS series of the same name, was born in Houston, Texas, and was educated in Canada, where he studied for the Roman Catholic priesthood, earning three degrees from the University of Toronto. For the past twenty years, he has worked as a counselor, a theologian, a management consultant, and a public speaker.*

# 2

# Extended Self

## Guide: Maureen Murdock

*"My own visit with my extended self has been
a source of beauty, inspiration, and strength...."*

## Introduction

It is possible to take a glimpse into the future, to perceive a
sense of one's place in the whole through contact with the
extended self. The extended self is that part of self which has
already reached its full potential, the blueprint that has been
actualized. Doing "Extended Self" may produce an insight
that may change your attitudes about yourself and the world
around you. You may thereafter see reality a different way,
value life from a new perspective, and lose fear about the
future.

## The Journey

Close your eyes and begin to follow your breath in and out
of your nostrils. Now give yourself the suggestion that with
each exhalation, your body becomes more and more relaxed.

In this exercise you will call forth from the future your
extended self. The you that has reached his (her) full potential and wisdom. Once again, open your dominant hand to

receive the hand of your wise being. Feel the texture of his skin. When he appears, begin to interact with him, learning from his life experience and wisdom. Notice the environments he shows you. The colors, sounds, smells and tastes. You will have five minutes of clock time equal to all of the time you need to be with your extended self. Begin....

Now bring your extended self to meet your little child. The three of you sit down together; your extended self is holding you, and you are holding your child. Feel the union of the three, the love and wisdom and power of all aspects of your self.

Now release both your child and extended self into their time/space dimension, knowing that you can call upon them again and that they will always be there for you....

Now become aware of who you are in your wholeness. In a moment, I will count to ten. Join me at the count of six, opening your eyes at ten, feeling relaxed and alert and ready to record your experience. One... two... three... four... five... six... seven... eight... nine... ten.

*Maureen Murdock is an educator, therapist, and artist. She discovered the benefits of guided imagery with her own children and then took these techniques into her classroom and therapy practice.*

*From* Spinning Inward: Using Guided Imagery with Children for Learning, Creativity Relaxation *by Maureen Murdock copyright © 1987 by Maureen Murdock. Reprinted by arrangement with Shambhala Publications, Inc., 300 Massachusetts Ave., Boston, MA 02115.*

# 3

# Forgiveness

## Guide: Joan Borysenko, Ph.D.

*"Forgiveness is the exercise of compassion and
is both a process and an attitude."*

## Introduction

"In the process of forgiveness, we convert the suffering created by our own mistakes or as a result of being hurt by others into psychological and spiritual growth." Through the attitude of forgiveness, we attain happiness and serenity by letting go of the ego's incessant need to judge ourselves and others.

Dr. Joan Borysenko developed the following meditation as an adjunct to her other work in the forgiveness process. Before you go into this meditation, she suggests you decide who needs forgiveness. However, she adds, do not be surprised if someone else appears. Dr. Borysenko also suggests beginning with small hurts, rather than starting with "your most vibrant enemy."

## The Journey

Take a deep breath and gently close your eyes. Give a few big sighs... sighs of relief... and see if your body wants to stretch a little... or yawn.

## Pause

Now pay attention to the natural rhythm of your breathing. Feel you body rise gently as you breathe in and relax as you breathe out.

## Pause

Every outbreath is an opportunity to let go... to relax a little bit more, to let your body sink down... and to feel the comfortable heaviness and warmth.

## Pause

And you can travel through your mind to the meadows of your innermost being... to a sunlit clearing fresh with the mild, fragrant breezes of spring.... As you breathe, you can relax into the warmth of the sun and feel the wind caress your body and ruffle your clothing... you can attune yourself more and more to the delightful sights and sounds and fragrances... the grasses, trees, and flowers... the birds and butterflies... the abundance of life in the meadow... and the sounds of the crickets and the wind in the trees... and you can feel the peace here in this special place... and the lifeforce of the awakening spring.

## Pause

And you can feel the lifeforce in your own body... feel it resonating with the meadow... feel it as joy.... And the meadow is a place of safety, truth, and peace... a place of wisdom within yourself where you can always come... and within the meadow are many special places you can discover... places where you can feel your own power... and places where you can feel especially cozy and safe.

## Pause

Around the edge of the meadow are openings to different paths — the life experiences you have had... paths over spacious, sunlit hills, and through dark, narrow valleys... paths through wooded labyrinths and vast open spaces... and each of the paths, whether high or low, is like a rainbow... for it has a pot of gold... a gift of learning... at its end.

Nestled in the safety of your own special place, you can look down into the paths of your life experiences... at relationships you've had with other people... (read in a slightly louder voice)... and choose one where anger, hurt, or guilt or some other emotion still blocks the way to forgiveness... and, in a moment, you will see a symbolic image of that emotion walking down the path to meet you at the edge of the meadow... to bring you the gift of its teachings.

## Pause

Bring your inner emotional messenger to the place of greatest comfort for you in the meadow. It may be a power-place or a safe-place. Since you have changed since you last contacted this feeling, you may want to make your messenger smaller or larger....

Settle down and bring the situation that needs forgiveness to mind now.... Ask you emotion how it protected you in that situation... and thank it for its help.... Ask it if there are other ways for you to feel safe now — ways that open your heart.... And ask what it has to teach you about the other person... and about yourself.

## Pause

Thank it for its teachings and return the favor by setting it free—letting its energy flow back to the lifesource—as a bird or a flower or a burst of light. Know that it will arise spontaneously wherever needed — free to form and to fade away... free to be spontaneously itself.

Feel the lifeforce in the sturdy shoots of new growth all around you.... Bow in your heart to the author of life... to yourself... to those who have exchanged love's teachings with you in the form of hurt... and know that you are both forgiven... now and forever.

And whenever you feel ready... taking your time... come back to the room, a little lighter than when you left.

*Joan Borysenko, Ph.D., is co-founder and former director of the Mind/Body Clinic, New England Deaconess Hospital, Harvard Medical School. She is currently president of Mind/Body Health Sciences Inc. which she founded with her husband, Myrin Borysenko, Ph.D. She holds a doctorate in anatomy and cellular biology from Harvard Medical School and is one of the pioneers of the new medical synthesis called psychoneuroimmunology.*

# 4

# Inanna's Descent

## Guide: Mary Ellen Carne, Ph.D.

*"Descend into the unconscious and
face the shadow without fear."*

### Introduction

This guided imagery introduces women to two significant
concepts of personal growth journey: the descent into the
unconscious and facing the shadow. It prepares and familiar-
izes women with this important aspect of psycho-spiritual
development. So often a "descent" or working with the
shadow creates a sense of fear, anxiety or foreboding when in
fact, it is an essential death/rebirth, psychologically reviving
process for women.

Through sharing and discussion, this experience creates a
better understanding of the descent process and shadow
work. It often brings up other descent experiences and the
feelings that surround them.

### The Journey

Find a way to make yourself comfortable. Close your eyes.
Begin by inhaling slowly and deeply through your nostrils.
Let the breath out through your nose slowly and completely.

Continue breathing in this manner, allowing your abdomen to rise as you inhale and fall as you exhale. As you breathe, allow yourself to relax.

Allow the feelings of relaxation to spread over your body. Allow your feet to relax. Allow your legs to relax, and let your muscles lengthen. Let the relaxation spread up to your pelvic area; continue to breathe deeply. With each breath, your body becomes more and more relaxed. Allow any worries or anxieties that you have to drift off. Release them—you don't need them here. Now let your abdomen and chest relax. Let the relaxation spread to your upper arms and down to your fingers. Now let your neck relax and your head relax.... You are experiencing a peaceful state of body relaxation and are at a time and space that are different from waking reality. You imagine and see things clearly in this place.

**Pause**

Imagine that it is dusk and you are on a path in a forest. It is warm, and you are wearing lightweight clothes. You are walking down the path. In front of you and behind you are others, walking the same path. The path winds gently downward and crosses a small stream with a bridge over it. You cross the bridge and are met by one of your guides, a very loved and trusted person. This guide may be familiar to you already or may be someone new. It is this person who will take you on the journey of Inanna's initiation descent and rebirth and you are eager to begin.

Your guide takes your hand, and you feel a sense of contentment flood over you as though someone has painted you with a source of supportive, healing energy that mingles with your own. Your guide leads you briefly through the forest until you reach the entrance of a cave where you feel a flow of cool moist air coming from the darkness. Surrounded by a nurturing, comforting sensation, you willingly follow your guide into the cave where you stop in front of a glowing red light. A voice tells you that this is the first of seven gates that you will encounter on your descent. You are told that at each one you will leave behind a worldly attachment, a role you play, a prized possession, an emotion or feeling that you hold for yourself or another. You are easily able to choose which one you will leave here. As you do, the gate takes on a particular shape that is symbolic to you. Notice what shape it takes. You are then easily able to step through your gate and continue your descent into the cave with your guide....

Off in the distance you see a glowing orange light signifying the second gate of descent. As you approach, the light seems to envelope you, and once again you are instructed to leave behind a worldly attachment. You take a moment to decide what you will leave behind. Once you do, the symbolic shape of the next gate appears to you. You move through it with ease and continue on your journey.

The third light you see in the cave is yellow, and you are immediately surrounded by its intensity. This gate seems a little more demanding as you are again challenged to leave behind one of your earthly attachments, a role you play in your life, a personality characteristic, a prized possession, an attitude or feeling you hold for yourself or another. The decision is a bit more difficult, but you are ultimately able to decide, and the symbolic shape of this third gate is revealed. You move through it effortlessly and proceed down your path.

The fourth light is a healing green radiance that permeates

your entire being and brings a sense of peace and calm. It affirms to you that you are on the right path, and when you are asked to leave another worldly attachment behind, you decide which one quickly, so that you may continue your descent. As before, the symbol of the fourth gate is magically revealed to you with your choice and you continue on with anticipation.

The fifth light is a brilliant blue spiral that encircles you with its energy and also asks you to leave an attachment behind, a possession, role or feeling to let go of in order to enter the next gate of your descent. The choice seems more difficult, but you are able to do so and feel much lighter in body and spirit. The symbolic shape of the fifth gate is revealed to you, and you once again feel the presence of your guide leading you downward on your descent into the cave.

The sixth area of light is a deep velvet-like violet light that wraps itself around you like a cloak and requests that another earthly attachment be left behind. It becomes more difficult to choose but it is possible and you do so. The shape of the sixth gate is revealed, and you slowly step through it, descending into the deepest darkness at the bottom of the cave. You remain in this darkness with your guide, accustoming yourself with all your senses to its blackness. You remain in the blackness for what seems to be a long time, taking this opportunity to just "be" because you are now free from worldly distractions and can experience for a few moments the simple essence of who you are. You find the experience of seeing yourself in your essence to be exhilarating. Take a moment to merge with the darkness and, without distraction, encounter your Self.

**Pause**

You now see a pinpoint of light glowing in the distance. It gradually moves closer as though it is trying to reach out to you. You sense that it is full of goodness and love, and mysteriously you see the outline of your own body begin to appear. The outline is filmy and smoke-like but it definitely has the size and shape of your body. Observe this body forming from your place in the darkness. It becomes more and more real and yet still transparent, full of air, as if it is made up of many tiny dots of light like the one you first perceived in the darkness. The white light continues to fill your body and at the same time it becomes more and more solid, more and more dense. Although it is still made of light, the dense material begins to predominate and your guide indicates that you can join with it whenever you are ready. Your essence, discovered in the darkness, easily merges with your body image and the sensation is wonderful. It is incredibly strong and calm; its energy is immense! All of a sudden you realize that it is this body shape that is the symbol of the seventh gate and by joining it, you have already gone through it and are winding your way upward out of the darkness. You continue walking out of the darkness of the cave using only a tiny bit of your new body's power.

Slowly, but with a new found lightness and power you move out of the cave, enjoying the new body and being your true Self. It feels incredibly light but grounded and centered at the same time. You take a couple of deep breaths to more fully experience this wondrous new body. It continues to feel more and more dense as you emerge until it is almost but not exactly the same as your old body.

Your path now leads you out of the cave where you are greeted by other new bodies and their guides, friends and other people who love you. You are aware of how your light radiates out to them and how theirs meets yours. Feel the joy and pleasure that this sharing of light brings to you. Bask in the energy and light that your essence and new body have drawn to you. Rest for a moment and let your new self reflect upon who you are and what this journey has meant to you.

## Pause

Now if you wish, allow your guide to help you see your reason for being here, letting it come into your consciousness. Don't be concerned if the whole picture isn't clear. It is a beginning, and you will receive more and more information as your new sense of "being" unfolds. Rest in this place, surrounded by your own supportive energy for as long as you wish. Let the new found energy and light all around you merge with the energy of your new body. Let it make you feel vibrant and whole. When you are ready to return to your usual state of consciousness, count slowly from one to three, and gently move parts of your body and return to the room. Open your eyes when you wish to do so.

*Mary Ellen Carne, Ph.D., is a masseuse, a stress management consultant, and a teacher of the Feminine Principal in Madison, Wisconsin. She teaches in an experiential manner that includes guided imagery and the sharing of personal experience through art, music, movement, and group discussion.*

# 5

# Keys

## Guide: Janet Doucette

*"Accept the many paths and many ways of
knowing and seeing spirituality."*

## Introduction

This journey came from a vision I had while visiting my
personal healing place. I use it in workshops on individuality
and personal knowledge. It helps one to see that their is not
only one right practice or belief. When you feel particularly
uplifted by a certain practice, or if you often urge others to
perform that same practice or belief, this meditation can
assist you in releasing the need to "prescribe" healing to
another. It frees us to pursue our own journey. Clients who
have used this imagery report that they experience a sense of
relief or greater understanding about the spiritual needs of
themselves compared to others.

## The Journey

Begin with mindful breathing and settle in. You see a flight
of stairs. Walk slowly down the steps, relaxing more and
more as you descend. Ten, nine, eight. Seven, six, five. Four,
three, two, one. You are now completely relaxed.

You are walking down a garden path. It is a beautiful garden with many wild flowers and abundant bushes and trees growing alongside the brick inlaid walkway. The walkway itself is constructed in an intricate pattern. The design is complex yet very beautiful to behold. At the sides of the path grow carefully manicured shrubbery. On the other side of the shrubs, flourishes a wild and untended garden of vibrant colors and flowers of unimaginable beauty. In this lovely setting, it seems as if all seasons are contained in one. Daffodils bloom beside roses; lilacs beside autumnal chrysanthemums. This is one of many strange and wonderful aspects of this garden. Many wild creatures walk through the garden in perfect contentment. Though some animals are the natural predator of others, they walk together in peace while within this magnificent place. You come upon a wrought iron bench and sit down to gaze at the garden around you. It is nice to look upon, but impossible to enter for there is no break in the thick shrubbery and no path through the wild undergrowth.

Soon a man, who is also walking along the path, joins you on the bench. He is smoking a pipe and wearing a dark hat. He is a Jewish man, and he's wearing a beautiful chain about his neck, from which is suspended a large key made of alabaster. Begin to walk together down the garden path.

Later you come upon a Buddhist woman who is quietly praying at a small shrine set into the wall of shrubbery that borders the great garden. She completes her prayers and stands up to face you. She, too, wears a key. It is bright gold and hangs from a golden chain that encircles her waist. You begin to discuss the keys. You talk about values and aspirations, beliefs and fears. It appears you have much in common but when you begin to talk about the manner in which one ought to seek goals and how one should behave in the world, you become bitterly opposed. You agree that these differences are to be expected in a world such as ours. You walk along together each believing, secretly, your own perception of life to be the only true way.

Soon you meet another traveler on the intricately patterned brick walkway. It is a Muslim gentleman. He wears an iron key on a strap around his waist. He joins you and he and the Jewish man fall into a heated discussion.

Before long, you meet a man from North America who asks if he can walk with you. He is a preacher of fundamentalist background and is very adamant about the copper key that he carries in his pocket. You begin spirited conversations with each other as you progress along the path. Soon your discussions and your capabilities to interpret scriptures and argue logically engross you fully, and you neglect to look at the beautiful scenery before you. The Buddhist woman says very little. She stops at the many pathside shrines to intone her endless prayers and hurries to catch up with your quick-paced group of dissenters.

Eventually, the group rounds a curve in the garden and struggles up a steep hill. There before you is a valley. In the valley stands a great walled city. It is the most breathtaking city any of you has ever seen. Speechless, and with great reverence, you approach the gate to the magnificent city. By the great sliding bolt on the gate are a series of locks. There is a gold lock and an alabaster lock. There is an iron lock and a copper lock. The Jewish man slides his alabaster key into the alabaster lock, confident of results. It does not release the bolt. He removes his key. The Muslim man set his iron key into the appropriate lock and turns it expectantly. Still the bolt remains tight in its hasp. With tears and great discouragement he removes his key. The Buddhist woman places her gold key in the gold lock without hesitation and turns the key. It does not release the bolt. Sadly she removes the key. The fundamentalist preacher steps forward and gives a short sermon. He makes a great ceremony of his copper key. He says, "It is evident to me that my key is the one that will turn the lock. It is clear that my key is the only true key to this gate since none of yours has opened it." He places his copper key in the copper lock and turns it. There is a creaking noise but the bolt remains fast. "I don't understand," he murmurs, "Can none of us enter the city?" Your reply is, "You are only partly in error. If there are four locks it must require four keys together to unlock the gate." Quickly, they place the four keys in the four locks and, crowding together, turn the keys. A grinding noise is heard and suddenly the bolt draws back. Your simple wisdom amazes them. They did not see the answer for themselves. They ask you about your wisdom.

You reply, *"I seek not to be a doer of deed, but to become the deed itself. Through my personal meditations I have reached that state of enlightenment. That is all. As for the keys,"* you continue, *"We are them and as for the gate, I don't see one."*

You walk into the city through the barrier that exists only in the mind.

*Janet Ware Doucette used guided imagery and cross-cultural healing techniques in workshops and support groups in order to enable others to experience their higher selves. A profound near-death experience in 1986 left her with an awareness of her ability to heal ourselves.*

# 6

# Search for The Beloved

## Guide: Jean Houston, Ph.D.

*"In all great and mystery traditions, the central theme,
the guiding passion, is the deep yearning
for the Beloved of the soul."*

### Introduction

This process allows you to experience, first through a guided
meditation and then through a powerful ritual, the experience of the search for the Beloved and the union with that
deep force within you. In different ways you will experience
this in each of the journeys presented in the last part of this
book, for all of sacred psychology ultimately speaks to this
quest. Here we experience it in and of itself. While each part,
the guided meditations and the ritual may be done sepa-
rately, they are most powerful when done together. Everyone participating in the experience should have read the
preceding text, or one person should read it first to the group
as a whole. Ample time must be allowed for the fullness of the
experience. Preparation and reading might be done before
dinner and the actual process begun in the evening. I have
found doing this at night most effective.

In the guided meditation the initial imagery is drawn from
archetypal forms which have haunted the Western imagination, helping to lead you into deeper levels of the journey.

Then the imagery enters into the search for the Beloved using classical images and situations common to the Celtic mythos.

The ritual of crossing the threshold to the realm of the Beloved is derived from my speculations on the little we know of the rites of *pothos* at Samothrace.

## The Journey

Sit up in a comfortable position and follow your own breathing, all the way in and all the way out, and all the way in and all the way out, and all the way in and all the way out, and all the way in and all the way out....

(When the participants are fully relaxed, begin the next stage.)

You are walking in the snow... in what seems to be a wasteland. The trees are few and sparse and bare....

It is a light snow.... Your footprints etch themselves in high relief.... And as you walk, you pass various strange scenes. On the left, you see a priestess with a golden lion standing between a black and a white marble column.....

And as you walk farther, you see a dwarf juggling with golden triangles.... And as you keep walking, you come upon a scene in which demons are tormenting a man on a tightrope....

Continuing to walk, you see a woman crucified upside down.... Continuing to walk, a naked androgyne discourses to you about the nature of love....

Continuing to walk, a skeleton in armor riding a black horse comes up to you, bows to you with great dignity, and hands you a golden chalice.... You continue to walk and you find yourself in a cosmic zoo with animals and creatures from all over the galaxy.... Continuing to walk a company of deaf mutes are performing the story of your life....

You now find yourself at the edge of a marsh of quicksand. You walk along this marsh of quicksand, and somehow pulling your feet up, you manage to get across....

Now you find yourself in a quiet forest where a bird in a tree says to you, "Your Beloved is in one of the towers of the white castle yonder."

And ahead you see a glorious medieval castle with two tall white towers from which are flying banners, and you run toward one of the circular towers....

You don't know which the Beloved is in, but you choose one, and you run up and around and up and around and up and around and.... Doors slam behind you, and you know they are locked but you don't care, you are so in yearning of the Beloved. You continue to run up to the top of the topmost tower, and the Beloved is not there....

And the doors are locked behind you. But over in the opposite tower you see or sense the Beloved of your soul, who is similarly caught there yearning for you.

You have a minute or so of clock time, equal subjectively to all the time you need, to find out what happens next. Begin....

And down on the ground, somehow you find the Beloved,

and your joy, in each other and with each other, is enormous...

But then a wind begins to come up and play around you, a gentle wind.... But gradually it becomes stronger and stronger and even more violent.... And the wind picks you up and hurls you away from the Beloved... and a great whirlwind hurls the Beloved in the opposite direction....

And you are separated and lost, and you can't find the Beloved.

And there comes along a giant hundred-pound porcupine, limping, badly wounded, and the porcupine says to you, "If you would carry me on your back and help me get away from the hunters, I will try to help you find the Beloved." So you pick up this giant animal with its terrible pointed quills and you carry it on your back in search of the Beloved.

You have a minute of clock time, equal subjectively to all the time you need, to find out what happens next. Begin...

And at the time that you are nearly at the place of the Beloved, a rain begins, a strange rain.... And the rains pour down and become torrential. And the little rivulets become mighty streams which become rivers... and the porcupine is washed away.... And the rain becomes acid rain, and it eats away at your complexion, at your body, making you look horribly ravaged, ugly, looking much like a monster. And you wander through the world so very ugly, almost a monster, ravaged by the acid rains, and people fear you because of your terrible appearance.

You have a minute or so of clock time to experience the

wandering through the world in this state of ugliness. Begin....

You come finally to a great grove of trees with strange surrealistic shapes, exuding choking, noxious smells. The trees are known as the Trees of Madness, and you have to pass through this grove. But the trees scream at you all kinds of horrible things, as well as telling you to go in different directions.... They reach out to grab you, to slap you, and to tell you things about yourself that you wish you hadn't heard. To go through this grove is to experience pain and madness.

You have a minute of clock time to go through these Trees of Madness. Begin....

One day in your wanderings in search of the Beloved, you find yourself in a little mountain village where you set up a small shop.... And people begin to come to you for advice... because out of your pain and sorrow you have grown deeply wise.

And people begin to come from the villages around and from the countryside to get your wisdom, your counsel....

And you give it lovingly and freely, and you stay in this little mountain village, in your little shop, giving wisdom and counsel to all who come, for seven years.

You have a minute and half of clock time, equal to all the time you need, equal to the seven years spent there giving wisdom and counsel in your little shop. Begin....

One day an old woman comes to the shop and says, "Now it

is time for you to seek the Beloved in the chapel that lies between the twin valleys.... The Beloved is there in the chapel waiting for you."

And you say, "Oh, but I am so ugly, I cannot face the Beloved." And the old woman says, "No, look in the mirror. Look what your gift of so much loving wisdom has restored to you."

And you look in the mirror and your skin is clean and pure again; your beauty is restored to more than it was. And the old woman says, "You must leave now, it is important, the time has come. Many will try to stop you on the way because of your reputation....

"They will stop and ask you to give counsel.... People will desperately cry out, but it is the rule that you may not speak to them, regardless of how desperately they ask you.... You may not speak. You must stay silent on your journey to the chapel."

You have a minute of clock time, equal to all the time you need, to walk through the twin valleys with many people trying to get you to speak to them and help them, beginning now....

You come to the chapel or little temple, and you are filled with excitement.... For you feel certain that the Beloved is there. And you run in and you see the most beautiful bowers of flowers on the altar surrounding something.... And you run up hoping to find the Beloved nearby, and you see that the flowers are covering a coffin, a casket... an open casket.... And you look inside, your heart hammering in your chest.... And it is the Beloved... lying dead in the casket... and your grief is enormous.

You have a minute of clock time, equal subjectively to all the time you need, to experience the fullness of your grief. Begin...

In your grief, your senses have become more keen and you notice that there is carved on the coffin the words, "You who would save the Beloved must sacrifice yourself so that the Beloved may live."

And your eye falls upon a very, very sharp, beautiful silver knife.... And you know that the sacrifice must be total, it must be complete.... And so you begin to cut yourself apart with the knife... you rend yourself and cut yourself to many pieces.

You have a minute or so of clock time, equal to all the time you need, to do this, beginning now...

You are dead... you are lying there dead....

Your soul ascends and looks down at your body lying in pieces there dead....

But you also note that some of your blood has fallen upon the face of the Beloved. Gradually you see the Beloved gaining color....

The Beloved begins to breathe.... The blood, having fallen upon the Beloved, seems to be restoring the Beloved to life....

And you observe as the beloved comes fully back to life, sits up, gets out of the coffin, and sees you in all your separate parts lying there. And the Beloved picks up your parts and with love and reverence puts them back together again....

And your soul descends into your body.... And you are more complete than you have ever been, and your life is restored... And you and the Beloved have now the time of joyful meeting, recognition, and communion.

You have a minute and a half of clock time, equal to all the time you need, for the meeting of communion with the Beloved...

(After this time has ended, let the music continue as the participants take 10 to 15 minutes to write or draw in their journals or to share their experience in pairs.)

*Jean Houston, Ph.D., a pioneer in human development, internationally renowned scientist and philosopher, and past president of the Association for Humanistic Psychology, has conducted seminars and worked in human development in more than thirty-five countries. She is director of the Foundation for Mind Research in New York and is the author of more than ten books.*

# 7

# Soul Star

## Guide: Joseph G. Spano, M.D.

*"Experience harmony, balance, and wholeness and allow
yourself to touch your true identity and purpose."*

## Introduction

In this meditation, you are able to connect to the Source, the
Soul, or the Essence. It is self-healing in providing an experience of balance and wholeness. One is brought into spiritual service thus allowing one to touch into true identity and
purpose. This exercise came intuitively as a gift. I am aware
that others have come forth with similar journeys so the
information must have been disseminated simultaneously
for reasons that are apparent.

Use it any time you find that the world and personal ego have
been seducing you away from the true purpose and priority
of life. This soulful exercise is deceiving in its simplicity. It
connects you with your higher self, and in doing so allows
you to access your own wisdom, truth, and innate harmony.

## The Journey

Close your eyes and visualize a star above the crown of your
head, perhaps six, twelve or more inches. (The height de-

pends on what seems comfortable.) See diamond light rays that burst forth in all directions. And now repeat this invocation of power that invokes the soul energy.

"I am the soul. I am the light divine. I am love. I am will. I am fixed design."

Now see the star come spiraling down in a clockwise fashion. It passes around the crown of the head; violet rays of light are ignited in the crown. It spirals around the brow; indigo blue is evoked. As it moves downward, spiraling, it passes in front of the throat and sapphire blue becomes manifest. It moves downward around the heart, front and back; beautiful emerald green light is awakened and pulsates in the heart. It continues journeying down and around the solar plexus now; golden yellow, like the semi-precious amber, is brought forth and spirals on down to the lower abdominal area, the sexual energy zone. Now the light is fiery orange, as in a topaz or in an opal. It spirals down around the base of the spine, the root; ruby red light becomes manifest. It spirals on downward and turns around like a comet spiraling through the center of the body, starting at the base of the spine and goes through each of the areas as it ascends burrowing a tunnel or tube of brilliant white light. It comes up through the chest, through the neck, through the head and out through the top of the crown and the star rests once more up above the crown.

### Pause

And now repeat the process. The star spirals down around the crown, the brow and the back of the head; throat, front and back; chest, front and back; solar plexus, and lower abdomen, front and back; and down around the base of the spine.

It turns and comes upward into the base of the spine through the center of the body, spiraling upward it passes once more through the upper abdomen to the chest, throat, head and out through the crown. Now there is a tube of brilliant white vibrating light from crown to root.

### Pause

And now repeat: "The sons of men are one and I am one with them. I seek to love, not hate. I seek to serve and not exact due service. I seek to heal, not hurt. Let pain bring due reward and light and love. Let the soul control the outer form, and life, and all events, and bring to light the love that underlies the happenings of the time. Let vision come and insight, let the future stand revealed. Let inner union demonstrate and outer cleavages be gone. Let love prevail. Let all men love."

### Pause

Now take your star and connect it with all the stars of all the souls that together serve mankind so that there are interconnecting triangles of light that cover the planet. Send light and love into all the troubled areas of the world. Let love and light replace the darkness. Conscientiously think of the troubled spots in the world and send love and light — unconditional love, free of any judgments or contingencies. Now bring back the star. Send it forth to your loved ones. Let the star enter the crown of your loved ones and filter through liquid golden crystals, filling that individual with love and light. Actually visualize that person filling with the healing energy and love, manifest by liquid gold. The crystals penetrate into every tissue. Bring the star back above your own crown, then bring it down into your own crown. Take golden rays from the star and see the liquid crystal of gold and light enter into your brain and permeate your entire body, cleansing, feeling, harmonizing, nurturing. Feel yourself being overwhelmed by the energy of joy, the manifesting energy of love. Feel it in your fingers, toes, scalp, extremities, abdomen, chest, heart, lungs, throat — your entire being.

**Pause**

From the point of light within the mind of God, let light stream forth into the minds of men. Let light descend on earth. From the point of love within the heart of God, let love stream forth into the hearts of men. May Christ return to earth. From the center where the will of God is known, let purpose guide the little wills of men. The purpose that the Masters know and serve. From the center, which we call the race of men, let the plan of love and light work out and may it seal the door where evil dwells. Let light and love and power restore the plan on earth.

The star now takes place once more up above the crown of the head, beaming brightly, ready to serve you at any time in the future.

*Joseph G. Spano, M.D., a practicing physician for twenty-two years, is a board certified specialist in internal medicine who subsequently trained in gastroenterology. He is also a metaphysician who leads a music and meditation group in Naples, Florida, now in its twelfth year.*

# 8

# Source Connecting

## Guide: Loryn C. Martin

*"Experience the power of love that is constant within us."*

## Introduction

Human beings are looking for happiness. Much time is spent looking outside of ourselves for what we think makes us happy, and time after time we are disappointed because what we thought was the answer, wasn't. Eventually, we learn that true everlasting happiness can only come from inside ourselves. Connecting with the Source or desiring to have only the peace of God within as our highest desire brings us closer and closer to what true lasting happiness is. This meditation was created to give you a technique to get in touch with that wonderful power within that can truly bring happiness and peace when desired and applied. May this meditation lead you to knowing who you truly are!

## The Journey

Visualize yourself on a round gold platform. On the floor of the platform is a button labeled The Source. Push the button. A beautiful ray of light comes on from above and the platform begins to lift up towards that light. You continue to lift higher and higher, and higher and higher. The light seems to get brighter and brighter, and you feel yourself becoming filled with more and more light and the energy becomes finer and finer.

### Pause

Call forth the spiritual helpers of the light and visualize them assisting you as you move forth into higher and higher vibrations moving towards the Source of all light. Feel your desire to become one with The Source, to feel your connection. Allow your desire to lift you still higher and higher. Stop for a moment and allow to come forth into your mind anything in your life that has stopped you from feeling your oneness with The Source. It may be someone you need to forgive; it may be feelings of guilt or unworthiness. It may be a fear that you have to leave the pleasures of earth. It may be a combination of things. Just allow them to come forth.

### Pause

Look at them and feel your desire for The Source to be greater than holding on to these things. Then feel your desire to let them go and see them leaving you, asking your spiritual friends to help carry them off to be dissolved into the light. Now feeling freer, feel your desire to connect with The Source and feel the platform once again moving upward going higher and higher and higher and higher. Feel and see yourself moving into more and more light *until you feel yourself absorbed by the light* and allow yourself to just be. Feel the energy in your heart expand.

### Pause

At this point, feel The Source breathing you. Feel the oneness of just being. Stay in this energy as long as you like. Before coming back, remind yourself of your desire to have this energy be more and more a part of your life.

Then when you are ready, bring the energy back with you and bring your awareness back into the room. Bring yourself back gently and slowly.

*Loryn C. Martin is a teacher, Ro-Hun therapist, healer, psychic writer, and artist residing in Colorado and Hawaii. She began her training at the age of 19 and has, during the past 16 years, assisted others along the path as she continues her own spiritual growth.*

# 9

# Tree of Life

## Guide: Fred Wass, M.H.S.

*"Feel the energy of God and nature flowing through your life."*

## Introduction

The "Tree of Life" is a journey that puts us in touch with the flow of nature within us. It gives us a deeper insight into the many changes of our life and gives us the confidence to surrender with trust to the gradual process of transformation. Through this journey, we begin to become aware that there is a slow, sure movement of grace and energy that will vitalize our whole being if we trust the flow of God.

## The Journey

During this imagery, feel free to move as you are instructed. These gentle movements will be optional, but sometimes they help a person become more integrated in the image and to deepen the work with their own body.

Breathe very gently. You are now breathing into a small seed located deep within your heart. The seed is planted deep in the soil of life. Relax. Feel the smallness of the seed. Go within the seed, explore the darkness.

## Pause

Breathe. As you breathe a little more deeply now you can feel the first stir of life within the seed. Deep within the soil of earth, something is beginning to happen. There is a life stirring within the seed. Something is wanting to be born, to come anew, to live. Ever so gently, a small sprout begins to break forth from the seed. The sprout begins to grow upward to the earth, feeling the moisture on either side. Gently reach up with your fingers now, as you count one... reach up... two... reach up... three... reach up... four... reach up... five... reach up. Now take a deeper breath. As the seed is about to break forth through the soil, you can feel the resistance but there is something within you that needs to come forth. Lift up your shoulders now and push through the top of the soil.

You are now in the light for the first time. You can feel the sun forming your little sprout. You can feel the wind blowing you back and forth as you begin to move your body, gently swaying back and forth, back and forth, back and forth. Now breathe again and begin to stretch forth your legs as the trunk begins to grow... up, away from the earth toward the sky... grow, growing to the ankles, growing, to the knees. Little nodules on the trunk of the tree begin to form, growing, up through the groin, through the stomach, growing, growing, through the heart. As branches begin to form, stretch out, let them grow. Breathe into the branches, stretch ever so gently, stretch, stretch, stretch. Notice the tiny little leaves they are forming. Feel the swaying of the wind, touch them, see them, see that deep green of the newborn leaf. See the delicacy.

Continue to grow up, grow and stretch through your throat. Begin to lift your head a little bit more, stretching your neck upward to the sky. From the head, the branches begin to form ever so flourishing. The leaves begin to cover the beautiful head, the trunk is now reaching up, and the top of your chakra crown is now opened. Look up into the sky; look at the clouds above. You are a part of the clouds. Earth and sky are joined. You belong here. You are beautiful. On the very crown chakra a little white blossom begins to open, ever so slowly. Each petal is beautiful, each petal is reaching out, feel... feel... feel... your fingers reaching forth, reaching upward to the sky. Feel again the wind brushing against the new petals of your new flower. Hear the rustle of the wind against all your leaves and branches... feel... feel... feel... the new life of a tree that you are.

## Pause

Now you begin to feel a new sensation upon your forehead. A drop of gentle rain, cool, wet, refreshing. And then another drop, and still another drop of rain. The raindrop begins to slide down your face as tear, down the trunk of the tree. As the rain increases, the drops become a steady stream flowing down over your face, your chest, your back, your stomach, down through your legs, down deep into the roots of the very earth, the soil. In the roots, the rain begins to follow each of your roots, deeper and deeper into that soil. The water begins to mix with a light, golden sap, the vital life, the food of your new life. Gently you begin to raise the sap up, up, up into your ankles, into your legs. Feel the nourishment, the strength, breathe into your legs now. Mingle with the sap. Feel the thanksgiving and the joy of the legs, of the trunk, of the tree that you are. Let this sap flow through, around and around mixing with all the organs of your body, your upper and lower intestines, into the spine, and into the chakras moving ever so slowly.

Then as you take a gentle deep breath, the sap moves into the heart; it begins to penetrate deeply. Inside the gold light of the sap is mixing deeply until you can see the bright gold color that is forming now within your heart; and throughout the life of the tree, the life of the soul. The sap moves forward through the arms, through all the branches; the leaves begin to breathe in the sap. Feel it going into each leaf throughout your body. Each of the cells are anxious to receive their nourishment and their new life. The sap continues to rise upward to your throat, liquid honey gently coating your throat. All the sore places in your body are being healed from this gentle, healing golden sap of life. Now it is moving through your mouth, you can now taste the sweetness of a nectar not known before, as it touches your tongue. You wet your lips with the golden sap.

Now as the raindrops mixed with the sap begin to move up into your nostrils, you can smell this gentle, freshness of the new order and the new sap mixed together. As it moves into your eyes, you can see the crystal drops. Each drop is different. Each one a different crystal of life, the wonder, the miracle of the rain, the sap that is yours. Then as it moves into your ears, it begins to circle the inside and outside; then you can hear the little drops and the great drops. You can hear the rushing of the sap from the water. Sometimes deep within itself like a gentle water flow, sometimes just a drop of rain. Then as it moves up into the brain, it begins to go through the cells; it begins to mix with all the electro-motor organs of the brain, all the messages that are sent back and forth, all the thoughts become empowered by the sap. Gently stop for a moment to rest, to take a slight drink of refreshment from the new rain.

**Pause**

Thoughts that are fearful, can now be released because they are energized by a new life. Let go now of the worries, the fear, the anger; let go. Open up the brain now as it moves into the very highest crown chakra to be regenerated. The crown chakra begins to open and from your brain and your heart and soul, you sing forth. Raise your hands and sing, "hallelujah, thanksgiving, praise. I am a beautiful tree, I am a beautiful person, I am." Looking around, you see other trees, each different from you, some taller, some shorter, some wider, some thinner; each has a different geometric design; each gives glory in its own way. Each is holy by being the tree, by bringing forth its own fruit, its own blossom, its own leaves. It only has to be true to itself. Wave your branches to the other trees and they wave back in unison.

Now feel a drop of snow, cold, wet and for the first time you begin to notice that your leaves are now dropping and you are becoming bare, but it is different kind of cold, a different kind of bareness. You know that this is a time of relaxing, a time of waiting, a time of sleeping, a time for gentle hibernation. Allow yourself this privilege of letting the leaves go and just being with the snow. Gently the cold flakes begin to run down your trunk melting to ice water and beginning to cover the ground below. Now as far as you can see there are just a few leaves left in the beautiful white snow that covers the earth. Send your leaves wherever you wish — they now become of a new earth, waiting again to create a new season. Follow one of your leaves to some person you love. They see the brown leaf. It appears to be dead, but is only waiting again to become part of their new life. Send your leaf anywhere you wish, to someone you resent, someone that has been difficult, some pain in your life. You can send a leaf with a message from your heart.

## Pause

Feel the cold upon your trunk. Begin to feel the loneliness and some of the desolation of winter, but you can also see the sun that is starting to bring forth the spring. See the snow melting and gradually one by one, little, tiny leaves begin to spring forth. Once again the process of your new life begins. So whether you are having good moments or bad moments, this is your process. It is all part of your destiny. Now stand tall again with all your leaves flourishing from the green of another spring, waving, waving, rejoicing, rejoicing, breathing deep, laughing, playing, being a part of the universe. You are a beautiful tree; you are a beautiful person. You are you; you are the only tree of its kind and relaxing in the beautiful tree that you are, you give thanks.

*Fred Wass is the former clinical director of Willoughs and the Palm Beach Institute. He has a degree in theology from the University of Loulain in Belgium and a master's degree in psychology from Johns Hopkins University in Baltimore. He is a specialist in stress and addiction related problems and is now in private clinical practice of psychotherapy and director of the Southwest Florida Center for Counseling in Naples, Florida.*

# 10

# White Cloud

## Guide: Halcyone Therriault

*"Answers may come to you when
your mind becomes relaxed and quiet."*

### Introduction

I created this journey so that I could relax my body and let
healing come into my organs. Healing comes in many forms
— mainly physical and mental. Mental healing seems very
important before physical healing can occur. Relaxation of
the mind opens the body for healing. The ocean seems to
have a calming atmosphere for most people, and the water
and gentle sun are very soothing. All these aspects create a
good background for the journey, which is short and can be
enjoyed anywhere.

### The Journey

Relax yourself as comfortably as you can in your chair. Relax
your jaws and your shoulders. Take a couple of deep breaths
and just relax.

Let's take a short journey down to the beach. When you
arrive, take off your shoes. Now, walk over to the ramp
leading to the beach but stop at the trash container and

deposit into the can all of your fears and anxieties. You don't need them on this journey today. In fact, you don't ever need them again.

Now you are ready to walk down the ramp onto the sand. It is early enough in the day so that the sand is cool and there are very few people on the beach. Go on down to the water's edge. Now that you are there with your feet in the water, turn to the north (which is to your right) and start walking.

Feel the gentle water lapping at your feet. It is early in the day and the sun is shining. It is warm on your head but not hot. You feel the warmth moving down gently from your head into your shoulders, like a giant massage on your shoulders. It moves on down into your arms, on down your back. Just feel the warmth of the sun massaging your back. Gently circling over your pelvic area and all through your internal organs. Your intestines, your liver, the pancreas and the spleen are — relaxing any kind of tension you might feel in your stomach area. Now, the warmth has spread to your thighs, on down to your knees, into your lower legs and into your feet — filling your whole body with a natural warmth that is very, very relaxing. Continue walking with this light energy, that the sun has given to you. Feel it in your arms and in your legs, in your entire body. Remember that all your fear and all your anxiety has been left in that trash can. Since your feet are in the water, you gradually start feeling a delightful coolness take over your body. Just stand facing the water and enjoy the coolness and the light breeze. Now, look up into the sky and there's one, little, lone cloud up there. It's your cloud. It is light and fluffy and very full of wisdom. If you have a question, present it now to the cloud. Take time now to be quiet and see if an answer comes back to you. Just close your eyes and listen. Remember that your are totally at peace.

The universe is always full of wisdom, and if we take the time to be quiet, sometimes our answers will come back to us. Perhaps the answer will come from your own heart.

**Pause**

Feel your own personal energy. Your body, because of the sun's warmth and the water's coolness is now in perfect harmony. You are at peace with yourself and the world. You can continue on with the day in this perfect harmony.

You don't want to leave this perfect setting of the beach but now we will turn around and head back . Don't pause at the trash can, let someone else take your troubles and dispose of them. You are a free spirit now. You are free of fear, free of anger, free of depression, free of disease, free of pain. You are full of life and energy. Peace be with you.

Now open your eyes, stretch your arms, neck, shoulders and your entire body.

*Halcyone Therriault has survived her challenge with cancer much longer than experts had expected, and she attributes this to major changes she has made in her life. Meditation, imagery, relaxation, and medical care have extended her life with high quality. She no longer lives a life full of stress.*

# Healing

# 11

# Glove Anesthesia

### Guide: David E. Bresler, Ph.D.

*"This imagery provides a dramatic illustration
of the power of self-control."*

## Introduction

. In this two-step imagery exercise, first you learn to develop
feelings of numbness in your hand, as if it were in an
imaginary anesthetic glove. Next you learn to transfer these
feelings of numbness to any part of your body that hurts,
simply by placing your "anesthetized" hand on it. This
process, taught to me by William Z. Kroger, M.D., is a
symptomatic technique — that is, it reduces the physical
symptoms of pain without concern for the cause.

It is a useful alternative to analgesic medications, particularly
when discomfort is so intense that the patient cannot concentrate enough to use other guided imagery approaches.
"Glove Anesthesia" helps to "take the edge off" the pain
sensation, thus permitting the patient to explore other
aspects of the pain experience more fully. In addition,
"Glove Anesthesia" provides a dramatic illustration of the
power of self-control. When patients realize that they can
produce feelings of numbness in their hands at will, they also
recognize that they may be able to control their discomfort
too. This is profoundly therapeutic for pain suffers who feel

totally helpless and unable to affect their discomfort.

## The Journey

Before beginning, take a moment to get comfortable and relaxed. Sit upright in a comfortable chair, feet flat on the floor, and loosen any tight clothing or jewelry or shoes that might distract you. Make sure you won't be interrupted for a few minutes. Take the telephone off the hook if necessary.

Take a few slow, deep abdominal breaths. Inhale... Exhale... Inhale... Exhale... Focus your attention on your breathing throughout this exercise, and recognize how easily slow, deep breathing alone can help produce a nice state of deep, gentle relaxation.

Let your body breathe itself, according to its own natural rhythm, slowly, easily, and deeply. Now, close your eyes and begin the exercise with the signal breath, a special message that tells the body you are ready to enter a state of deep relaxation. Exhale... Breathe in deeply through your nose... And blow out through your mouth.

You may notice a kind of tingling sensation as you take the signal breath. But whatever you feel is your body's way of acknowledging the experience of relaxation, comfort and peace of mind that awaits you.

Remember your breathing, slowly and deeply... As you concentrate your attention on your breathing, imagine a ball of pure energy or white light that starts at your lower abdomen, and as you inhale, it rises up the front of your body to your forehead... As you exhale, it moves down your spine, down your legs, and into the ground...

Again, imagine this ball of pure energy or white light rise up the front of your body to you forehead as you inhale... And as you exhale, it goes down your spine, down your legs, and into the ground... Circulate the ball of energy around for a few moments... Allow its circulation to move you into even deeper states of relaxation and comfort...

Each time you inhale and exhale, you may be surprised to find yourself twice as relaxed as you were a moment before... Twice as comfortable... Twice as peaceful... For with each breath, every cell of your body becomes at ease... Let go as all the tension, tightness, pain, or discomfort drains down your spine, down your legs, and into the ground... Continue to circulate this ball of energy around for a few moments...

Remember your breathing, slowly and deeply from the abdomen... Now take a brief inventory of your body, starting at the top of your head working down to the tips of your toes... Is every part of your body totally relaxed and comfortable? If so, wonderful, enjoy how good it feels.

However, if there is still any part of your body that is not yet fully relaxed and comfortable, simply inhale a deep breath and send it into that region, bringing soothing, relaxing, nourishing, healing oxygen into every cell of that area, comforting it and relaxing it.

As you exhale, imagine blowing out right through your skin any tension, tightness, pain or discomfort from that area... Again, as you inhale, bring relaxing healing oxygen into every cell of that region, and as you exhale blow away right through the skin and out into the air any tension or discomfort that remains in that area... In this way, you can use your breath to relax any part of your body which is not yet as fully relaxed and comfortable as it can be...

Breathe slowly and deeply, and with each breath, you may be surprised to find that you have become twice as relaxed as you were before and that you are able to blow away twice as much tension and discomfort as you did with the previous breath... Inhale... Exhale... Twice as relaxed... Inhale... Exhale... Twice as comfortable...

Now with your eyes remaining closed, imagine that a small table is being placed in front of you. On the table is a bucket filled with a sparkling clear, odorless fluid. Can you see it in your mind's eye? Is the bucket a metal or plastic one? What color is it? Imagine it as vividly as you can.

The fluid in this bucket is an extremely potent anesthetic, one so powerful that it can easily penetrate any living tissue, quickly rendering it insensitive to all feeling. In a moment, at the count of three, I will instruct you to lift your right or left hand, and then dip it into the imaginary bucket up to wrist level. Really do it, really lift your hand, for if you proceed through these actions as if they are real, you may be surprised to discover that the relief you experience will also be real.

One... two... three... Now raise your hand and slowly dip it into the bucket. Feel your fingertips tingle as the anesthetic is quickly absorbed. When you feel the tingle, or any change in your fingertips, slowly begin to dip your hand deeper. Feel the numbness go up to your knuckles, across your palm and the back of your hand, and now, all the way up to your wrist...

The skin on your hand may be beginning to feel constricted and tingly, and as the anesthetic penetrates even deeper, you may begin to notice a numb, wooden-like feeling in the muscles of your hand and fingers.

As the numbness seeps even deeper, the bones themselves may lose all feeling. Gently swirl your hand around in the bucket to ensure the deepest possible penetration of the anesthetic solution. Sense any remaining feelings in your hand moving out the tips of your fingers, floating down softly to the bottom of the bucket.

Continue to swirl your hand around for as long as it takes to achieve total anesthesia, a deep feeling of tingling numbness.

In a moment, at the count of three, I will instruct you to remove your hand from the bucket and gently to place it directly on any part of your body that hurts. This will permit you to transfer the deep feelings of numbness from your hand into the area of your discomfort, and in exchange, any tension, tightness, pain, or discomfort will flow from this area back into your hand... You will then re-dip your hand into the bucket to remove these uncomfortable sensations, and to refill your hand again with the pain-relieving numbness.

One... two... three... Now remove your hand from the bucket and place it directly on the part of your body that hurts. Imagine all the deep feelings of numbness from your hand streaming into every cell of that area, and simultaneously, picture your hand beginning to absorb all the discomfort from that area.

Notice that the same numbness that quickly developed in your hand is now permeating the painful part of your body. Can you sense the skin constricting? Are the muscles losing all feeling as the numbness penetrates even deeper? Can you experience your hand becoming filled with the uncomfortable sensations you once experienced only in that affected area?

Slowly rub your hand around the area until you feel you have transferred as much anesthesia and absorbed as much of the discomfort as you can. You may be surprised to notice what an immediate difference this has made.

Now, dip your hand once again into the bucket to repeat the exercise. Swirl your hand around in the anesthetic solution to allow the transferred feeling of discomfort to drain out through your fingertips and flow down to the bottom of the bucket.

At the same time, feel your hand react once again to the anesthetic solution, deeply absorbing it through the skin, into the muscles and bones. Once again, fill your hand completely with the feeling of tingly numbness. It will probably take much less time to achieve this state than it did the last time, but continue to swirl your hand around for as long as it takes, whether it be a few seconds, or even a minute or more.

Soak up as much numbness as your hand can hold, and when you're ready, place your hand back on the area of discomfort.

Once again, let the tingly, relaxed feelings of numbness seep deeply into every cell of the area. If there is any remaining discomfort, drain it back into your hand. Gently rub your hand over the area, transferring these feelings as fully as you can, until you are ready to dip your hand into the bucket once again and repeat the process.

Continue to move back and forth from the bucket to the affected area at your own pace. You may repeat the transfer process as many times as you like at your own pace. For each time you repeat it, you will be able to experience an even greater amount of comfort and relief in the affected area.

Each time you repeat the transfer, it will become easier and easier for you. Continue to practice now at your own pace...

When you are ready to end this exercise, simply shake your hand briskly to quickly return all the feelings to it that existed before the exercise began.

After completing this session of glove anesthesia, you may be surprised to notice that you will feel not only relaxed and comfortable, but energized with such a powerful sense of well-being that you will easily be able to meet any demands that arise.

To complete the exercise, simply open your eyes and take the signal breath... Exhale... Breathe in deeply through your nose... Blow out through your mouth... And be well...

*David E. Bresler, Ph.D., former Director of the UCLA Pain Control Unit and former professor in the UCLA Medical and Dental Schools and the UCLA Psychology Department, is currently in private practice in Santa Monica, California. He is the executive director of the Bresler Center Medical Group.*

*Reprinted by permission of David E. Bresler, Ph.D. from* Free Yourself From Pain, *P.O. Box 967, Pacific Palisades, CA 90272.*

# 12

# Healing Prayer

## Guide: Louise L. Hay

*"The use of love makes me feel good.*
*It is an expression of my inner joy."*

## Introduction

This beautiful short meditation is powerful in its simplicity, and it makes a soothing daily meditation. Enjoy and feel the love that it releases within you.

## The Journey

Deep in the center of my being there is an infinite well of Love. I now allow this Love to flow to the surface. It fills my heart, my body, my mind, my consciousness, my very being, and radiates out from me in all directions and returns to me multiplied. The more Love I use and give, the more I have to give; the supply is endless. The use of love makes me feel good; it is an expression of my inner joy.

I love myself; therefore I take loving care of my body. I lovingly feed it nourishing foods and beverages. I lovingly groom it and dress it and my body lovingly responds to me with vibrant health and energy. I love myself; therefore I provide for myself a comfortable home, one that fills all my needs and is a pleasure to be in. I fill the rooms with the vibration of Love so that all who enter, myself included, will feel this love and be nourished by it. I love myself; therefore I work at a job that I truly enjoy doing, one that uses my creative talents and abilities, working with and for people that I love and that love me, and earning a good income.

I love myself; therefore I behave and think in a loving way to all people for I know that which I give out returns to me multiplied. I only attract loving people in my world for they are a mirror of what I am. I love myself; therefore I forgive and totally release the past and all past experiences and I am free. I love myself; therefore I love totally in the now, experiencing each moment as good and knowing that my future is bright and joyous, and secure for I am a beloved child of the universe and the universe lovingly takes care of me now and forever more. As so it is.

*Louise L. Hay, a metaphysical teacher and bestselling author of nine books including* You Can Heal Your Life, *has assisted thousands of people in discovering and using the full potential of their own creative powers for personal growth and self-healing.*

# 13

# Image of Wellness

## Guide: Martin L. Rossman, M.D.

*"Imagery is not only a set of tools for healing, but for preventing illness and living the highest quality daily life."*

### Introduction

Imagery skills can assist your movement toward wellness whether you are ill or currently healthy but desire an even fuller, more satisfying life. Imagery can help you solve practical problems, develop insight into others, improve your relationships, enhance your self-confidence, and help you reach the goals you set for yourself.

This imagery may serve as a blueprint or a goal to work toward, or it may serve as an affirmation of the health and well-being you already experience.

### The Journey

Begin as usual by taking a comfortable position and loosening any restrictive clothing or jewelry.... Take a couple of deep, full breaths and let the out breath be a real "letting go" kind of breath.... Imagine that with each exhalation you begin to release and relax any unnecessary tension you feel....

Allow your breathing to take its natural rate and rhythm... allow yourself to relax more deeply with each breath... allow the gentle movement of your chest and abdomen to take you more deeply inside.... Invite your body to relax and become comfortably supported by the surface beneath it...

As you relax more deeply, your mind can become quiet and still.... When you are ready, imagine yourself going inside to that special inner place of deep peacefulness and concentration you have visited before... take time to notice what you see there today... what you hear in this special place... an aroma or a fragrance that is there... and especially that sense of peacefulness, quiet, and security that you feel in this place.

This is your special inner place... a place you can come to for rest... for healing... for learning things that will be helpful to you.

Take some time and find the spot where you feel most deeply relaxed, most quiet, centered, and connected to the natural healing qualities of this special place.... Allow yourself to sense the healing qualities of this place supporting and nourishing your vitality and movement toward greater wellness.

### Pause

When you are ready, allow an image of you enjoying wellness to arise.... Welcome the image as it forms in your awareness, and allow it to become clear.... Take some time to notice what you observe.... It may look like you or be a symbolic representation.... What does it look like?... What is it wearing, if anything?... How does it move, how does it hold itself?... What is it's face like?

How does the image seem to feel?... Notice what this image is doing.... Are there other people, places, or things in this image of wellness?

What are the qualities this image embodies?... What is it about this image that conveys a sense of wellness to you?... Are there particular qualities that seem to be intimately connected with its wellness?

### Pause

When you feel ready, imagine yourself becoming the image.... Notice how that feels.... Notice your posture, your face... especially notice the feelings of well-being you experience.... Imagine looking out of the eyes of the image.... How does the world look from here?... What is your world view?... If you had a motto, what would it be?

### Pause

Imagine looking back at yourself.... How do you look from this perspective?... What do you think of this person you are looking at?... How do you feel about this person?... Is there anything you know that would be helpful for this person to know?

Become yourself again, and continue to feel the qualities and feelings of wellness within you.... Observe the image of wellness once more.... Does it seem different in any way?... Is there anything you understand about it now that you didn't before?

Is there anything that stands in the way of your moving more toward that experience of wellness in your daily life?

What issues or concerns arise as you consider this?... How might you deal with them in a healthy way and take a step toward greater wellness today?

When you are ready, slowly return to your waking consciousness, remembering what has been important to you in this experience.... When you come fully awake, take some time to write about your experience.

*Martin L. Rossman, M.D. is a general practice physician in Mill Valley, California. He has taught imagery techniques to several thousand patients and health professionals during the past twenty years. Dr. Rossman is a Clinical Associate at the University of California Medical Center at the University of California Medical Center in San Francisco and a member of the scientific advisory council of the Institute for the Advancement of Health.*

# 14

# Integrating
# Disowned Parts

## Guide: John Bradshaw

*"Reunite the essential parts of yourself."*

## Introduction

Perhaps no one has done more pioneering work in healing toxic shame than Virginia Satir. I remember the first time I saw her work with a family. Her validation and nurturing of each person was something to behold. As she performed her mighty mirroring, I could see each person accept herself a little better. As that happened, the family moved closer together. The work was so beautiful, I actually wept while watching her work.

In her book, *Your Many Faces,* Virginia presents the core theory of a technique that is used by therapists all over the country. It is commonly called the Parts Party. I've seen this exercise adapted in various ways by different schools of therapy. In what follows I will give you may own variation of this very powerful exercise. My belief is that this work is best done with a group of people. It has more impact.

## The Journey

Close your eyes.... Let your mind focus on your breathing

Spend two or three minutes just becoming mindful of your breathing. As you breathe in and out begin to see the number seven appear on a screen. It can be a black number seven on a white screen or a white number seven on a black screen. Focus on the number seven. If you can't see it clearly, imagine that you finger paint it or hear a voice say seven in your mind's ear, or do all three if you can. Then see, finger paint, hear, the number six; then five; then four, etc., down to the number one. As you focus on the number one, let it slowly turn into a stage door and see it slowly open. Walk through the stage door and see a beautiful little theater. Look at the walls and the stage.... Look at the closed curtain.... Sit down in a front row seat and feel the fabric of the seat.... Make if your favorite fabric. Feel it as you sit down. Get comfortable.

**Pause**

Look around again and make this theater be any way you want it to be. Then see the curtain beginning to open.... Let yourself feel the excitement that goes with such an opening. As the curtain opens see a large sign covering the wall of the stage. It reads "The (put your name) Parts Review." Think of some part of yourself that you really like and see some famous person or someone you know well who represents that part walk out on the stage. I like my humor and I see Johnny Carson walk out.... Hear a resounding applause. Then think of another part of you that you really like and repeat the process. I like my charismatic speaking ability and my honesty and I see John F. Kennedy walk onto the stage. Repeat this until five people are on the right hand side of the stage. Then think of a part of yourself you don't like and see that part walk onto the stage as personified by a famous person or someone you know. I don't like my sloppiness and disorganization and I see a very unkempt friend of mine walk onto the stage. Hear a resounding boo as if there was an audience there. Then think of another part that you don't like. I don't like the part of me that is cowardly and afraid and I see a person whom I imagine to be Judas Iscariot walk onto the stage. Finally, after five parts you hate or dislike or reject are standing on the left side of the stage, imagine that a wise and beautiful person walks to the center of the stage. This person can look like an old man with a beard or a radiant youth like Jesus or a warm nurturing mother or whatever.... Just let your wise person appear.... Then see her walking off the stage and coming to get you.... As she approaches, notice whatever strikes you about her.... Then hear her invite you to come up on the stage and review your many parts.

Walk around each person who represents a part of you; look her in the face. How does each part help you? How does each part hinder or limit you, especially your undesirable parts? What can you learn from your undesirable parts? What can they teach you? Now imagine they are all interacting. Imagine them at a table discussing a problem. Think of a current problem you have. What does your humor say about it? How is that helpful? How does it hinder you? How does your disorganization help you? What would happen if you simply didn't have this part? What would you lose? How would you like to change the part you want to reject? Modify that part in the way it would be more beneficial.... How does it feel to modify that part?...

Now go around and repeat that procedure with every single part. Modify it until it feels right for you. Then walk up to each part and imagine that part melting into you. Do this until you are alone on the stage with your wise person. Hear the wise person tell you that this is the theater of your life. This is the place you can come and review your many selves from time to time. Hear the wise person tell you that all these parts belong to you, that each has its own complementariness in your psychic balance. Make a decision to embrace your selves; to love and accept and learn from all your parts.... See your wise person walk away. Thank her for the lesson. Know that you can call on her again.... Walk down off the stage. Be aware of yourself sitting in the theater looking at the stage whereon you play out your life. Let your mind see each of your newly modified parts float by and feel yourself as one whole organism with many aspects and interdynamic parts. Speak out, hear yourself saying, "I love and accept all of me." Say it again. Subvocalize it as you get up to walk out of your theater. Walk through the theater doors. Turn around and see the number one... a black number one on a white curtain or white number one on a black curtain. Finger paint it and hear it if you can. Or do any of these. Then see the number two and do the same thing. Then the number three, start feeling the life in your fingers and toes. Let it come up through your legs. See the number four and feel your whole body becoming alive. Then see the number five and know that you are coming back to your normal waking consciousness. See the number six and say I am becoming fully conscious — feel the place where you are and when you see the number seven, be fully restored to your present waking consciousness.

*John Bradshaw, author of best-selling* Bradshaw On: The Family *and television host for the PBS series of the same name, was born in Houston, Texas, and was educated in Canada, where he studied for the Roman Catholic priesthood, earning three degrees from the University of Toronto.*

*Reprinted with the permission of the publishers Health Communications, Inc. Deerfield Beach, Florida from* Healing The Shame That Binds You *by John Bradshaw copyright date 1988.*

# 15

# Kinesthetic Body

## Guide: Jean Houston, Ph.D.

*"... Restore your inner and outer sensing..."*

## Introduction

In this process we will be using what I have called the "kinesthetic body" (from the Greek: *kinema* – motion, and *esthesia* – sensing). It is the body image encoded in the motor cortex of the brain, but which is experienced as the *felt* body of muscular imagination. The experience of the kinesthetic body is familiar to athletes and musicians who rehearse inwardly when not actually performing their respective skills. Many of them seem to have an experience in this kinesthetic rehearsal almost as vivid as the actual physical engagement. Sometimes, too, watching an artistic or athletic event will so engage you that you will feel kinesthetically that you are actually participating in the event. Thus the boxing match or the adventure movie or the tenor reaching for high C can leave you physically elated or exhausted.

If you are working alone, you will want to read these instruction onto an audiotape, pausing to leave time for the movement. If you are the guide in a group, you will want to remain constantly alert to the time required by the participants for the movement.

## The Journey

Before you begin, stand up, get a sense of your body as it is, at rest, quiet, ready to experience.

Now raise your real right arm over your head and feel the stretching of muscles throughout the arm and the torso as you do so....

Now lower your arm. Repeat this process of raising your right arm several times, remembering to concentrate on the feeling of the movement within the body.

Now sense your right arm as clearly as you can with your muscular imagination... and then stretch this *kinesthetic* right arm — that is, the arm of muscular imagination – over your head, trying to experience it as vividly as you sensed the real one. Now lower your kinesthetic right arm.

Alternate several times between stretching with your real right arm and your kinesthetic right arm....

Do the same thing with your real left arm and your kinesthetic left arm, always remembering to experience your kinesthetic arm with as much reality as you had when stretching your real arm.

Do the same thing, alternately stretching your real and kinesthetic arms.

Let your real shoulders make circular movements forward, down, and around, like spinning windmills, remembering to concentrate on the feeling of the movement.

Now do the same thing with your kinesthetic shoulders, trying to feel the same forward circular movement that you felt with your real shoulders.

Alternate between real and kinesthetic movement.

Do the same thing kinesthetically.

Alternate.

Now with your real body, make a fencing lunge to the right. Come back to center. Repeat this several times.

Now lunge to the right with your kinesthetic body. Come back to center.

Alternate several times between your real and your kinesthetic body as you lunge to the right and back to center.

Do the same thing with a fencing lunge to the left.

Follow this sequence: Real body lunges to the right. Back to center. Real body lunges to the left. Back to center.

Kinesthetic body lunges to the left. Back to center.

Real body lunges to the left. Back to center.

Kinesthetic body lunges to the right and comes back.

Real body lunges to the right and comes back. Real body lunges to the left and comes back.

Now, at the same time, your kinesthetic body lunges to the

right and your real body lunges to the left. Back to center.

Now lunge with your real body to the right and your kinesthetic body to the left. Come back to center.

Now alternate lunging simultaneously with the kinesthetic body in one direction and the real body in the other. Do this a number of times.

Rest.

(Feel free to experiment with this process, utilizing as many different movements as you like. Movements can include jumping up and down in your physical body, followed by jumping up and down as vividly as possible in your kinesthetic imagination. Another kind of practice could involve going back and forth between the real and the kinesthetic bodies while raising and lowering your arms, spinning slowly in one direction and then in the other, and so forth. Gradually you will notice the sense of the kinesthetic body getting stronger until it is almost as vividly sensed as the actual physical body.)

*Jean Houston, Ph.D., a pioneer in human development, internationally renowned scientist and philosopher, and past president of the Association for Humanistic Psychology, has conducted seminars and worked in human development in more than thirty-five countries. She is director of the Foundation for Mind Research in New York and is the author of more than ten books.*

# 16

# Overcoming the Big Lie

## Guide: Wayne Dyer, Ph.D.

*"The society in which you find yourself is simply the stage upon which you are acting out your own miracles."*

### Introduction

In his book, *Real Magic*, Dr. Wayne Dyer promotes the theory that "we grow up believing so many limitations that after a while our lives actually manifest those limitations. We hear ourselves saying things that we accept as truth, when in fact they are misbeliefs that have turned into our truths. As long as you hang onto the big lie, the "truth" of these misbeliefs, you cannot become a person who experiences miracles, he explains. He continues to list five misbeliefs that he feels permeate our culture: 1) I can't help the way I am; I've always been this way, 2) It's my nature, I inherited who I am and it can't be changed, 3) My personality is controlled by my chemistry and metabolism, 4) My family is responsible for my personality, 5) I can't escape my culture and times.

The following may be used as a positive affirmation to recognize the "misbeliefs" in your life and learn how to become a person who believes in magic!

### The Journey

"I am a miracle!" Repeat this over and over to yourself until it is firmly planted in your mind. Be in awe of yourself. Producing miracles for yourself is about knowing within that you are already miraculous. When you know and feel the miracle that you are, you begin to also know and feel that nothing is impossible for you. You begin to sense that you no longer need to hang onto those five excuses outlined above, and in their place you substitute your new awareness. To overcome the big lie that your misbeliefs are the truth, you will need to equip yourself with new, empowering beliefs. You must come to know that you can choose the life you want to live. You can choose to make your life into a grand, ever-evolving work of art. The key is in your thoughts, the wondrous invisible part of you that is your spiritual soul.

You have come into this world housed for a while in a limited body. But you also have an unlimited mind. This mind of yours is unbounded, formless, and infinitely capable of creating any kind of miracle that it chooses, when it is fully honored and celebrated. It can occupy an ill form, grow up in a dysfunctional family, be in a shy depressed personality, have stuttering behavior, an average or genius IQ, and a host of phobias and fears if it wants, and it can even choose to believe that it has no choice in the matter and convince others of the same.

### Pause

Or, it can choose something else. It can use this infinite invisible force to create a miraculous purposeful person. With real-magic thinking you can leave behind the old conditioned hypnosis and see that there are those who have surpassed seemingly insurmountable conditions. Then you can use your thoughts to know that if one person can leave schizophrenia behind, and one can overcome manic-depression, and another can become a physician in spite of being told he was dyslexic or event retarded, then whatever force is flowing through them to allow those miracles, you can tap into it and use it to become the personality that you want to be.

Real-magic thinking says, "I believe it, I know it, and I will access my spiritual powers to do it. It is my intention!"

*Dr. Wayne Dyer is the author of numerous books including his most recent national best seller,* Real Magic. *Dr. Dyer is a psychotherapist with a doctorate in counseling psychology. He lectures across the country to groups numbering in the thousands and appears regularly on radio and television. Dr. Dyer lives with his family in southern Florida.*

# 17

# Perfect Health

## Guide: Mona O'Neal

*"When we begin to realize that we are more than our body, we can allow our mind to heal us."*

### Introduction

Although there are many wonderful healing meditations available, this one is different in that it calls forth feelings. I have found that emotions are the catalyst to the images we create. In this journey, we reach inward for the *feeling of perfect health*. This feeling, when held in the conscious mind, forms a new consciousness — a belief of one's own wellness, from which true healing is possible.

### The Journey

Find a comfortable place where you will not be interrupted for fifteen minutes and sit or lie down. Feel your body completely supported by the chair or the floor or the bed. Take a few deep relaxing breaths. As you breathe in and out normally, feel the air bringing in with it a pure white light that enters your nose and your throat and your lungs. Allow your breath to bring in more and more of this pure, white light into your lungs and from there out into every artery and even the tiniest veins in your body. Everywhere that the blood is taking oxygen from the air, it now takes this purifying and healing white light.

Feel the light moving within you. Feel the tingle, the gentle current bathing each area of your body... illuminating in every organ... regenerating every cell... flooding every atom in your body with brilliant perfection. Breathe deeply and naturally for a few more minutes while you watch each breath bring this healing light in and through your entire body.

If there is a particular area of concern within your body, bring it into focus now, and allow this healing light to surround and wash over and through it. Tell this place in your body, "I love you, you are free to be perfect now. All the darkness is gone." Maintain this feeling and the nurturing of that particular place in your body, for a few more minutes. Just let it melt into the light.

Know, and mentally repeat with me, "I know that this light which fills my whole being right now is pure and perfect healing light of God, the life force of pure and perfect spirit. God is light and in him is no darkness at all. This light is my light now and forever."

It is time to move your wonderful, brilliant light filled body down a path in the forest. The green leaves are dappled with sunlight, filtering down to the mossy path below. Feel the soft, cool air on your skin. Smell the richness of the soil. Hear the sounds of the forest teaming with life of every description. Breathe in that life deeply and breathe it out. Let this life flow freely through you. As you walk on, feel your brilliant light filled body exchange its energy and its love with all the forms of life you meet as you continue on the path. You are truly one with all of nature.

As you reach a sunny meadow clearing ahead, see a marker that says, "My Healthiest Day." Step out into the warmth of that wonderful day now. How old are you? What are you wearing? What are you doing with all that energy? Watch your body moving in response to your every command. How does it feel to be strong, vibrant and surging with life and vitality? Make a permanent image in your mind of this dynamic feeling, breathing it deeply into every atom of your body. Hold it there as you would before the focus of a camera and click the shutter of your mind. Release your breath but hold onto that feeling. The memory that produced that feeling was just a thought. The feeling it produced was not a *past* feeling. That feeling of health and vibrancy and alive-ness is real within you *right now*. That vibrant thought and that healthy feeling are clearly etched into your mind now, and you can recreate them any time you recall them.

Bring this dynamic energy with you back onto the forest path on the other side of the clearing. The cool shade feels soothing on your skin. Breathe in the quiet, restful peace and feel the crunch of fallen leaves and smooth pebbles under your feet as you walk on toward a small temple in a grove of stately evergreen trees. The sign here says, "My body, Temple of Wisdom." The door swings open gently as you approach and step inside. Here is a video theater with state-of-the-art technology and the film is ready. As the lights dim, realize that you *are* your "Body of Light," pure and perfect spirit, eternal, whole, perfect and complete, right where you are sitting. Know that the image on the screen is just of your outer physical shell of skin and blood, bones and hair, and the necessary parts to keep it functioning.

Watch the amazing processes that are going on. The breath comes and goes easily, naturally, bringing life-giving oxygen with no conscious effort from you. The blood takes oxygen and food to every atom without your supervision. Each organ knows precisely how to do its work without instruction to maintain a physical home for this third-dimensional experience called life. What a miracle!

Now ask your body what it has to teach you. Where are there blocks to be released? What am I holding back? What part of me needs more nourishment, more love? How can I be more flexible? How can I focus stress into power? When you have asked your own questions, wait for the answers. They will come. Take a moment now to watch on the screen and to listen for the information you need....

Do now what you are willing to do to perfect the image there. Ask for the willingness to move things around, erase mistakes and create the perfect image.

It is now time to go. If you have not received your answers, do not be concerned. They will come next time or in another way. Now bring your body of light up to the screen and step down into the physical form that is there. Let your image walk to the edge of the screen, merging with the body of pure light that you are and returning into this moment. Awake, alert and feeling fine.

*Mona O'Neal is a Religious Science Practitioner in Vista, California. She writes and conducts workshops on meditation, visualization, self-esteem, and personal growth issues. Her guided imageries, "Meditation in the Real World - 15 Minutes at a Time," are available on tape. Order form in back of this book.*

# 18

# Pink Bubble

## Guide: Shakti Gawain

*"This meditation is simple and wonderfully effective."*

## Introduction

This meditation explains the process by which you can enhance, expand, and enjoy your imagination. This creative tool is available to assist you in all aspects of your life. The following meditation is a lesson in "letting go" of your desires, which often fail to manifest because we hold on to them too tightly.

## The Journey

Sit or lie down comfortably, close your eyes and breathe deeply, slowly, and naturally. Gradually relax deeper and deeper.

Imagine something that you would like to manifest. Imagine that it has already happened. Picture it as clearly as possible in your mind.

Now in your mind's eye surround your fantasy with a pink bubble; put your goal inside the bubble. Pink is the color associated with the heart, and if this color vibration surrounds whatever you visualize, it will bring to you only that which is in perfect affinity with your being.

The third step is to let go of the bubble and imagine it floating off into the universe, still containing your vision. This symbolizes that your are emotionally "letting go" of it. Now it is free to float around in the universe, attracting and gathering energy for its manifestation.

There is nothing more you need to do.

*Shakti Gawain, author of the bestsellers* Creative Visualization *and* Living in the Light, *gives clear explanations and practical guidance for anyone who desires to develop their intuition and learn to follow it, using their creative abilities to the fullest.*

*Excerpted from* Creative Visualization, *©1978. Reprinted with permission of New World Library, San Rafael, CA 94903.*

# 19

# Sam & Sammy

## Guide: Suzanne McGlamery

*"Dolphin energy is respected as healing and peaceful."*

## Introduction

Dolphins have highly developed abilities to seek and detect through vibratory sensations, and so they became the guides for this journey, which was created while I was performing a mental, or intuitive, scan of my body for certain malignant cells. The idea is based on the concept that our bodies will give us the information we need and ask for.

## The Journey

You are safe, self-assured and in control. You are centered on the alignment of the body and aware of the illness that has temporarily invaded your body. It is time to destroy all of these bad cells. Use nature's tools to go through your body to locate and heal, with the forces of nature, the cells running rampant. These cells appear as shaded areas. See your body from above and take an x-ray of your body. Intuition and inner vision show you where the shaded areas are. The shaded areas are small dark spots about the size of a quarter. Envision your body as an ocean, wet, flowing freely. See the blood vessels in the body as rivers and streams. These rivers and streams travel from all points to feed into this ocean. Starting at the reservoir of the head you allow two creatures to come in. They are dolphins named Sam and Sammy. You see the dolphins swimming playfully and spontaneously; their bodies smooth and glistening as they swim back and forth, around and around. They travel the rivers and streams seeking out the malformed cells with their sonar. Your intuition shows them where to dispatch energy, focusing on the cells and cleansing the cells. You trust Sam and Sammy, letting go of all conscious feelings — just being with what's there at the moment. As they travel through and approach the malformed cells, they stop and surround them. The shaded area magnifies when the dolphins enter. With a beam of healing white light, they send out their zap. The white healing beam originates in their lower body and exits through their snout. Their zap quickly eradicates the cell. It lightens the entire shaded area. They jump for joy. The dolphins stay in the area until there are no shaded areas left. When they leave, they leave it clear of any malformed cells. Rest assured that, unknowing to you, their healing mission continues.

*Suzanne McGlamery is an interior designer and mother of four who is celebrating her twelfth year of good health following the diagnosis of breast cancer. She has practiced visualization faithfully over the years, and she believes its effects are very powerful.*

# 20

# Seed of Light

## Guide: Larry Moen

*"To see the light in yourself is to see beyond yourself."*

### Introduction

Striving for a state of enlightenment is a lifelong path attained most effectively by letting go of your thinking mind and listening to your heart. As you travel with the light, you become one with love, and you will see beyond this Earthly plane.

As you gain insight, you become aware of the importance of gratitude in the search for light. As you travel the path toward the light, you also discover freedom. You sense the openness of love. You see there are no boundaries, no temperature, no emotions or limitations. You discover new subtle feelings.

You will appreciate and support the human experience, but you will be drawn to the path that brings Eternal Light and joy. It is not always an easy path, but its rewards are freedom, reassurance, and love.

## The Journey

Begin by taking a few deep breaths, releasing tension and discomfort as you breathe out. Now be aware of all the different muscles throughout your body. As you breathe out, release any tension in your muscles, and let them become heavier and heavier as you become more and more deeply relaxed. Let a blanket of warm relaxation spread over your body, and let yourself sink down into that quiet place inside yourself. Your body is feeling warm, heavy, and deeply relaxed. Your mind is becoming calm and peaceful. You are ready to begin your inner journey.

Relax your breathing now and begin to imagine how you might release this physical plane and travel through your being toward the light. Who will share the light with you?

Begin now to visualize a guide who appears to help you achieve this oneness with love. See this guide handing you a book of wisdom. Notice how this guide looks, how the guide is dressed, and what mannerisms he or she expresses. Know that this guide will anchor your connection to the physical plane as you travel toward the light during this journey.

### Pause

For now, your body is unimportant. It constricts and limits you. Imagine placing your hand at your hairline above your forehead and gently removing your mask. Pull down your face mask from the top. Look inside. . . . What do you see?

**Pause**

Now visualize shedding your body. You see emptiness. You see vastness. Your body is still there in its physical form. You may choose at any time to wake up simply by taking a deep breath and saying to yourself — I am totally conscious now. And you will be aware of your entire body as always.

Now let us proceed gently. Allow your body and your skin to melt away like wax and fall to the floor. . . .(Be aware of your light body melting into the air.) As the bones and muscles and every material aspect of your being are laying on the floor, you notice a beam of white light, which represents your soul, or God, or Higher Power, or whatever title you choose. Your body has released itself and has opened up to this light of love and warmth within. Concentrate your efforts now on this white light and become the white light now. Visualize yourself as this beam of white light. You are the center of this beam. You are the core. You are the seed of light.

**Pause**

Notice the guide you have chosen to be with you. Your guide has already experienced what you are going through and is with you for reassurance, love, and compassion. Your guide nurtures you through your time of exploration and transformation.

You have become the seed of light. Allow yourself to float.

Allow yourself to experiment. The guide you have chosen is kneeling at your feet and will keep your resting body grounded. As you allow yourself to journey out into space, give yourself more and more freedom to leave.

**Pause**

Experience the joy and the love and the affection that is the true nature of all life. You are here to share and to spread the light. You are here to be one with the universe, to come into contact with all life forces and become united with them. To see clearly, is to be enlightened. . . . To be enlightened is to be intuitive. . . . To be intuitive is to gain wisdom. . . . To obtain wisdom is the greatest gift of all, for wisdom is what we all share.... To be united with all souls of the universe is the ultimate goal in our lives. So go in peace and be joyous. Release your physical body and embrace the light. Travel inward and travel upward with the light.

**Pause**

When you speak, speak of pleasant thoughts. Share your gift with all whom you meet. You are one with all living things. You are the light. . . . Be of light and become the love. . . . Become love, and you are united with all that exists.

# 21

# Wash Away Your Troubles

## Guide: William J. Ronan, M.S.

*"Learn the benefits of Hypno-Zen."*

**Introduction**

The technique described in this journey allows people "too busy" to practice meditation a chance to incorporate it as part of their daily lives. It needs nothing more than the usual daily activities most people experience.

**The Journey**

Close your eyes and imagine that as you wash your face and hands, you are washing away all of your troubles. Imagine that the dirt is being washed away, leaving your mind and body. Imagine it swirling down the drain. See it leaving you. Imagine starting everyday this way. Let the dirt and pain of your life be washed down the drain. See it being flushed away. Imagine that when you brush your teeth, you are cleaning out any uncomfortable words. Imagine when you wash your ears, you are preparing them to hear the beneficial things that are being said to you during the day, so that you can make the best decisions possible based on the information you receive. Imagine your eyes feeling more refreshed and seeing more clearly and precisely. Let it happen!

# Relaxation &
# Stress Release

# 22

# Angel Massage

## Guide: Margot Escott, M.S.W.

*"Dedicated to all the loving 'angels' who
practice the art of massage therapy."*

## Introduction

Too often "body work" is a neglected aspect of recovery from
addictions. This journey is especially helpful for recovering
food addicts. It is also useful for people who are just learning
how to use visualization for relaxation. Some experts feel
that much of the benefit of guided imagery derives from the
deep relaxation aspect. By focusing on each part of the body,
you will experience a sense of where and when you hold
tension and how to release it.

While this journey does not replace the valuable benefits of
therapeutic massage, it is a wonderful way to "mimic"
massage when none is available. It is also helpful in introduc-
ing people who have been reluctant for one reason or
another to try massage. This journey may be the first step
towards letting go of old fears and allowing yourself to
experience the healing power of touch.

## The Journey

This is a special experience, a time to let go and relax completely. Take a few deep breaths and let yourself go to that place where you feel relaxed and safe. When you're ready, close your eyes. As you breathe in, you breathe in a beautiful violet color, entering in through your nostrils and bathing your entire body with a beautiful violet color. As you exhale, you exhale a color that allows you to release any toxins, any anxiety, any fear. For the next few moments you inhale the beautiful violet color, bringing peace and relaxation to your body and exhale any tension or stress.

You become aware of a beautiful spirit guide, perhaps in the form of a shimmering angel. This is your special angel that has come to invite you to a place of rest and relaxation. With loving, gentle fingers the angel starts to massage the top of your scalp. Feel the top of your scalp being gently massaged with loving angel fingers, letting go of any unnecessary tension at the top of your head. Feel the massage going to your forehead, letting go of any wrinkles or lines or worry.

Lovingly and gently the angel massages your eyebrows and your eyelids, bringing peace and relaxation to your eyes, the area under your eyes, your nose, your cheeks, the area under your nose and around your mouth, perhaps allowing your mouth to relax even more and letting your tongue relax in your mouth. Now the angel gently massages your ears, lovingly caressing the outside and the inside of your ears. Now you feel those gentle fingers massaging away any tension in your jaw. So often we hold on to the jaw area. Let your jaw relax and let go. Know that as the angel massages the outside of your skin, the inside is also being bathed in a healing spiritual light. Feel the angel massaging the neck area, bringing release to the neck area and all of the muscles inside the throat.

Now feel your shoulders being gently massaged; letting go of any stress in the shoulders — the right shoulder, the left shoulder all the way down to the arms. The right arm, upper arm, elbow, lower arm, the wrist, the palm of the hand, and each individual finger of the right hand is lovingly massaged. You may notice now that your right hand and arm is very relaxed, perhaps feeling heavy and warm. Again, let your imagination take you to your left arm and feel the angel massaging the top of the left arm, the lower part, your elbow, the left hand, the palm of the hand, the fingertips. Your left arm now is very, very relaxed. Perhaps there is a pleasant, heavy warm feeling. Now allow your angel to massage the chest area, letting go of any tension and stress in the ribs inside the chest area. Feel those loving fingers permeate through to your heart area and imagine your heart area being bathed in a healing, luminous light.

And allow the angel to massage the abdomen so that the internal organs — the liver, the kidneys, the intestines also receive a healing massage. Feel the loving hand massage the buttock area, letting go of any tension or stress there. Feel the massage at the bottom of your spinal column and feel the angel massaging vertebrae by vertebrae, going up the spinal column, radiating through the entire back, bringing peaceful relaxation to the entire back area. Now begin to feel the angel massage your legs, starting at the top of the right leg. Feel those loving, tender fingers on the right hip and thigh, the right knee, behind the knee, the right calf. Feel those loving, tender fingers massaging the Achilles. And now, the ankle and the feet. The bottoms of the feet and the toes. Each individual toe receives a gentle massage, from your big toe of the right foot all the way to the little toe. You may notice that your entire right leg is becoming heavy, and there's a pleasant warm sensation through you right leg. Now feel the angel begin to massage your left leg, the left thigh, knee, calf, Achilles, ankle, foot, top of the foot, and again each of the toes of the left foot, so that your entire left leg feels peaceful and relaxed.

If there is any area where you're still carrying tension and stress, imagine your angel giving you more attention in that area. Now be aware of your angel guiding you in positive healing affirmations, allowing you to achieve your highest good and manifest all the beauty that you have inside. "I am at peace. I am calm. I love and accept my body as it is today. All of my body is operating peacefully and uniformly." All of the blood vessels and the cells, the skeletal and the muscle are functioning as they should.

If there's any area where you need extra love and attention, give your own affirmation to that part of the body now. In a moment your angel will be leaving. Know that you can bring back the angel of relaxation and heavenly angelic massage merely by closing your eyes, relaxing, breathing in the violet color and breathing out anything you don't need right now. As we count from one to three you'll find yourself becoming more and more awake and alert, feeling refreshed and at one with your body, your mind and your spirit. One, two, three.

*Margot Escott, M.S.W. is a social worker in private practice in Naples, Florida, where she uses visualization and guided imagery for stress management, pain control, and recovery from addictive illnesses. In 1992 she received a national grant from The Humor Project for her work on the Humor Cart at Naples Community Hospital. She presents workshops throughout the United States on "Healing with Humor and Play," "Discovering Your Inner Child," and "Visualization for Success."*

# 23

# Anger Release

## Guide: Jule Scotti Post, M.S.

*"Release your anger and move into
creating what you want for yourself."*

### Introduction

This journey was created because anger is an issue for so
many people. In Chinese medicine, the emotion of anger is
associated with the wood element. This is the element of the
springtime of growth, creativity, and vision. The imagery
reflects the movement through anger release to the creative
vision that is free to arise from within when we are no longer
blocked by unhealed anger. Many people have found it is
helpful to have an explanation of the flow of energy around
the cycle of the elements according to Chinese medicine;
their emotional patterns make more sense to them.

This imagery gives people permission to feel and release this
anger. It is best used in conjunction with other approaches
that facilitate outward expressions of anger that have been
held inside, perhaps for years. Directing your anger towards
a positive outcome increases the healing potential of this
process.

### The Journey

90

Take this time for yourself — to heal, to release, to relax and attune yourself to your inner being. Begin by bringing your attention to the lower part of your body, from the waist down. Now as you count slowly from one to seven, tense all the muscles in your stomach, lower back, thighs, calves, feet and toes. Hold this tension. As you count down from seven to one, gradually release this tension so that all the muscles from your waist down to your toes become very deeply relaxed.

**Pause**

Now bring your attention to the upper part of your body, from your waist up. As you count from one up to seven, tense all the muscles in your chest, your back, your arms and hands, your shoulders, your neck, your head and face. Hold this tension. As you count down from seven to one, gradually release all this tension so that all the muscles from your waist up to your head become very deeply relaxed.

**Pause**

Now that your body is feeling deeply relaxed, picture yourself, in your mind's eye, in a situation that makes you feel very angry. See the situation clearly. Perhaps there are people involved. Notice where you are, and what you are saying or hearing said, if appropriate. Let yourself move fully into the time of this experience. Now be aware of how you feel this anger in your body. Perhaps it is a churning in your stomach, a tightness in your throat, or a strong pressure in your head. Sometimes when we are very angry we feel we want to cry.

**Pause**

When you have released your anger, you may feel ready to move towards forgiveness. If so, visualize the person(s) who elicits your angry feelings. Now see them completely surrounded by light. Repeat to yourself the phrase: "I forgive you and I forgive myself." Continue until you can say it from your heart. Feel the relief forgiveness brings to your inner being.

**Pause**

Now it is time to let go of anger. It is time to leave behind those feelings that were keeping you stuck, blocking your growth. Let yourself move to another time. To springtime in a beautiful flower garden, surrounded by blossoming cherry and apple trees. As you walk down the brick path between the flower beds, you see a collage of color, of all your favorite flowers. You look to see which ones are there. As you breathe in deeply, smell the air thick with the sweet fragrance of blossoms and flowers; listen to the birds singing. Now you come to a beautifully carved wood bench. Sit here quietly feeling the hard strength of the wood, the smooth texture of its surface. Take in the peacefulness of the garden. Let your mind rest on thoughts of the future that you would like to create for yourself when you are free of angry feelings that cloud your inner vision. You have the power to decide, to choose, to plan your own growth. Release your creative energy and enjoy whatever comes to you.

**Pause**

Gradually begin to bring yourself back now to your body, to the room around you, to the day, the time of the present moment. As you open your eyes remember the calling of your inner visions and go into your life with renewed strength, rooted in your inner being, growing up to the light.

# 24

# Empty Jar

## Guide: Liz Bachtel

*"Safely and respectfully hold your thoughts and feelings until you are ready — or if you are ready — the choice is yours."*

## Introduction

This guided journey is effective for those times when focus and centering are necessary, but events of the day, stresses, or problems prevent us from getting clear. Through practicing "Empty Jar," you can respectfully put aside thoughts that keep you from productivity, facing tasks, or relationships. This journey was created to help myself and other students through the rigors of graduate school where we had too many pages to read and papers to write. This imagery provided a safe place to store my thoughts and feelings in order to journey out and get the job done.

## The Journey

First, uncross everything... legs... arms... hands... loosen anything that feels tight or constraining... collars... belts... shoes... jewelry. Keeping your spine straight, your shoulders relaxed, your feet making contact with the earth, allow the chair to support your body. As we go within to focus on the breath, I invite you to allow your eyes to close....

Gently now, bring your awareness to your breathing... begin to relax now as you breathe in and out... in and out.... Notice the wonder of your breath... cool against the back of your throat as you breathe in... warm as you breathe out... observe... relax... breathe.

As you grow more relaxed, you breathe more deeply, more slowly. Allow your breath now to move to other parts of your body... to find and to dispel your tension.... Your neck and shoulders hold so much... breathe in and with your next breath... breathe out that tension... arms, hands and fingers that do so much... breathe in appreciation of what they do and breathe out that tension.... Move now to your chest.... Breathe in gratitude for your heart, your lungs... breathe out any tightness.... Move gently now to your belly... allow it to be soft... let your breath move up from your belly... breathe out deeply from this intuitive part of yourself.... Notice buttocks and allow this chair to support you.... You don't have to do a thing... breathe in rest and relaxation.... Notice legs, thighs, knees, calves, ankles... how well they have carried you today.... Breathe in "thank you...." Breathe out their tiredness. Be aware of your feet, toes... how strong and supportive they have been... allow earth now to support your feet that have so well supported you... breathe deeply and relax.

As you breathe now, allow your breath to move lightly over your entire body dispelling any remaining tension. You relax more and more deeply with every breath.

Very gently, now... move to your mind... your third eye.... Visualize, if you will... a clear glass jar. It is empty. Observe yourself now as you unscrew the lid and remove it. Look closely at this empty jar, become aware that it is waiting to be filled. Take now the burdens, the busyness of your day... your activities... your work... your many tasks... your errands... your travel... your apprehensions... your anxiety... your cares... your pain.... Observe now as one by one you place them into the jar. Continue now to fill the jar with any remaining bit of your day. Carefully and deliberately now, replace the lid on the jar. Give the lid one extra turn.

Breathe deeply now and observe that you stand and begin to carry the jar toward a door. Open the door. Outside, on the front step is a large shiny aluminum trash can. Open its lid now and place your jar inside.... Know that you may dispose of it now and forever... or return for it at another time, if you wish.... Put the lid back on the trash can... turn from it... walk back through the door. Lock the door and return to your chair.

Become aware once again of your breathing.... You are in the here and now... ready to be fully present... refreshed... relaxed... in body and in mind...

Breathe quietly now for a few more moments and as you feel ready... begin to make small gentle movements.... Let your body begin to stir... and when you are ready... open your eyes.

*Liz Bachtel has a master's degree in holistic counseling, and she is currently engaged in full-time studies toward a doctoral in clinical psychology. She especially enjoys working with adolescents and with women's issues.*

# 25

# Letting Go

## Guide: Karen Carnabucci

*"A way to gain new awareness about yourself, your work, and your emotional attachment to others."*

## Introduction

This imagery was created for an experiential stress reduction workshop program for student assistance teachers and counselors who work with high-risk youth. However, it can prove helpful in teaching anyone the process of "letting go" of attachments to work or emotionally to others.

## The Journey

Close your eyes and begin to breathe deeply and evenly. Allow your body to let go of the tension that you have been carrying, beginning with your hair and scalp.... Letting go now in your forehead and eyes, moving to your jaw and letting go, then to your neck and letting go....

Let go now in your shoulders, your upper body, your arms, elbows, and fingers. Move down now to your stomach and abdomen... again letting go. Then let go in your pelvis and genitals....

Continue to let go now in your legs, knees, ankles, feet, and toes, and as you continue breathing, you feel relaxed and open to the next step....

In your mind's eye, see the face of a person with whom you have had difficulty letting go, mentally or emotionally.

### Pause

See this person now, noting the expression on his or her face, how he or she is dressed, and notice how you feel now as you face this person. How does it feel emotionally?... What do you feel in your body and where in your body?...

Ask yourself now how willing you are to let go of your attachment to this person and for what period of time.... Is it for today, for this weekend or for a longer period of time? Notice what feelings are connected to this question and the feelings regarding your answer.

### Pause

Does this person speak to you or have any message for you? Do you feel a need to answer? Say now whatever you need to say to this individual.... Notice if there is a reply and take a moment to decide if you need to say anything else.

### Pause

Surround this person with a bubble of light. Notice the color that you select for this light and how it feels to have this person surrounded by that bubble...

The bubble becomes a balloon and the balloon and the person in it drifts farther away from you. You become aware that the bubble is attached to a string or cord that is attached to you. Note the color, quality, construction, and strength of the cord.... Note, also, how this string or cord is attached to you and how it feels to be attached in such a manner.

**Pause**

Now is the time to cut the cord that attaches you to the other. Notice how it feels for you to consider making this cut....

Do you need to say anything else to this person before you cut? Is there a reply?

**Pause**

Cut the cord now, and as you do, notice how it feels emotionally and physically to take that action.... Allow yourself to breathe into these feelings now, and validate them as real and important to you at this time.

When you feel ready, bring yourself back to this room and open your eyes.

*Karen Carnabucci is a therapist specializing in experiential thera-pies, including psychodrama, family sculpture, and imagery, in her work with adult children of alcoholics and dysfunctional families. A former newspaper writer and editor, she is a consulting therapist at Caron Family Services, affiliated with the Caron Foundation, an internationally recognized drug and alcohol treat-ment center in Wernersville, PA. She recently collaborated on a book,* Intimacy, The Quest for Connection.

# 26

# Magic Carpet

## Guide: Karen M. Thomson, Ph.D.

*"An imagery journey that provides a 'mini-vacation."*

## Introduction

Without ever leaving your home, you can use this journey to "get away" from it all. And you are sure to return refreshed, rejuvenated, and at peace. It is wonderfully simple to connect with our inner peace when we take the time — at least once a day — to leave cares and responsibilities behind and journey, using the imagination, as far away as we care to go. When we re-enter ordinary reality after having made the journey, we can handle our lives with renewed vigor. You may use "Magic Carpet" as a vehicle for an enchanted journey far out into the cosmos.

## The Journey

Stretch out on the floor with your feet about two feet apart and your toes rolled away from each other. Place your hands about two feet from your body, palms up. From the base of your spine to the top of your head, you are in a straight line and are feeling very relaxed. This is a rest position which in Yoga is called The Sponge, or The Corpse, and in this

99

position, you are completely relaxed.

Go into very slow, deep breathing. As you inhale, count... slowly... to the end of the inhalation. Hold the breath to half of the count you had on the inhalation. When you're ready to exhale, count to the same number of your inhalation. Before inhaling again, count to half of the inhalation. For example: Inhale one... two... three... four... five... six... Hold... one... two... three... Exhale... one... two... three... four... five... six... Hold... one... two... three. Keep the concentration on your breathing and breathe for as long as you like. Allow the floor to support you as you, with every breath that you take, enter into a deeper and deeper state of relaxation and also a greater sense of awareness of a very peaceful feeling that you are beginning to experience.

### Pause

As the meditation continues and you enter into an altered state of consciousness, know that you can come out of it at any time simply by opening your eyes.

Feeling very peaceful and completely and totally relaxed, imagine filling and surrounding yourself with a beautiful white Light which will remain with you, protecting, guiding, blessing and healing you. Where there is Light, there can be no darkness. You are feeling so relaxed that you feel very, very light, as light as a feather, in fact, lighter than a feather. The feeling is more as if you were like a helium balloon, so light that you could gently float up toward the ceiling. Imagine yourself now on a Magic Carpet which is lifting you up, for you feel that you are gradually and gently moving up toward the ceiling, floating up. There is no fear, for you are completely protected in pure white Light in this very airy state of consciousness. You are so light that you now float through the ceiling and the roof, and up above the trees and into the sky. If you like, you can look back to where you've just come from and the roof and the tree tops are gradually getting smaller and appear as they would appear if you were in an airplane.

## Pause

You stretch out on your Magic Carpet as you glide up, up, up and now move through a cloud. You emerge from the cloud and feel the warm sunshine on your face, and it now warms your entire body. Every cell in your body breathes in this warm, gold Light that balances, heals, and rejuvenates every cell in your body. You are so high up now that you look back toward Earth, and it appears as a beautiful ball of light. See Earth now surrounded in a beautiful rose pink Light.

## Pause

When you're ready to come back, feel the Magic Carpet beginning to make a slow descent as it floats to and fro ever so gently back toward earth. There is a beautiful soft, billowy cloud which you gracefully and ever so quietly move down through. The tops of the trees are becoming visible as you look over the side of the Magic Carpet, which continues to descend slowly. As your roof comes into view, you feel an immense gratitude for the Magic Carpet ride. It has been a "time out" for you and you are returning relaxed, free, ready to meet your responsibilities and obligations. Feel yourself now peacefully coming down now through your roof and gently taking your place on the floor where you started your journey. Take a deep breath and be aware of your body and the fact that it has been energized, rejuvenated, rested and is ready to go now where you need to go. Take a deep breath, open your eyes, and continue to be at Peace!

# 27

# Medicine Place

## Guide: Janet Doucette

*"Within each of us is a special place —*
*a medicine place — where peace and beauty exist."*

## Introduction

In this journey, a private place of healing and peace is created. It is where one may go to experience the whole self. The catalyst for this journey was a garden that kept appearing in my personal meditations. With it came a feeling of complete peace and the perception of myself as a whole. By beginning with and returning to this place, many people have said that their imageries are easier to understand and more quickly assimilated because the garden is a familiar place. I believe it assists the person in "owning" the complete journey, and this choice of words is very positive. Many people discover that as they progress spiritually, this garden changes along with their personal growth.

## The Journey

Begin with mindful breathing. Sit straight with the spine erect, hands placed gently on your thighs. Settle in as you breathe in and allow the breath to spiral down, around and through you, nourishing your cells and organs, replenishing the blood and lymph system. Relax and release the toxins and the tension accumulated during the day. Release them with the exhaled breath, out into the white light, where they are absorbed. Sense your chakra energy centers opening one by one, spinning freely in a clockwise fashion.

You are walking down a hallway with many doors. Pause at each door and look it over carefully. Choose the door that beckons you. Notice its material, color, shape of door knob. Open the door and walk down the stairway. Ten, nine, eight steps. Seven, six, five, four steps. Three, two, one step more; now stepping onto a beautifully tiled parquet floor.

### Pause

Take a deep breath and then release it. Be mindful of the breathing, staying in the present, watching, accepting what comes to you. There is a mist gathering about you and the quality of feeling is light, intelligent, joyful. You may take time now to change your clothing or your appearance. When you are ready, step out from the cloak of mist. See before you a high stone wall. There is an open gate in this stone wall through which only you can pass. It is the gateway to a magnificent and eternal place. Walk through the gateway now, stepping over the boundary between worlds. And now before you is a special place, a garden of your spirit where everything you plant grows and continually blooms or bears foliage. There is a bench in this garden. Please sit on this bench. It may be of stone, wrought iron or wood. Look at it carefully and run your fingers across it. Take note now of your surroundings, your plantings and their essential order or random wildness. Notice what you have planted and where. You may hear water falling from high rocks, or bubbling down a shallow stream. This magical place of peace and symmetry is of your creation. No one may change a thing here. And no one may enter against your wishes. Take care to be mindful of the breath. See yourself as a being in constant outer vibration and yet with inner stillness. Hear the sounds of birds, water, wind and tree branches whispering about you. Then focus on that strange silence within.

### Pause

As you breathe in the healing white light of your medicine place and release the tensions or anxiety which may have surfaced, concentrate on that particular silence within. Grasp it with your intent, your curiosity, your respect. Like a tunnel of darkness surrounded by light, the silence beckons you. Deeper you go, touching walls inlaid with crystal, signifying your clear mind and single purpose. The silence is all around you, touching you like soft cotton balls, pushing on your aura, joining you. It is perfect peace. As you experience this silence, totally accept its stillness, its unvarying sense of peace and quietude. Above your head a falling star streaks across the heavens. It plummets to the earth and sends out a radiant beam of light that shimmers like a wave of heat and envelopes you in a conscious quality of feeling. Recognize this feeling, find words that express the quality of this sensation.

### Pause

Come back to consciousness and realize with a clear mind that you can return to this medicine place whenever you want. As you flex your wrists and stretch your legs, breathe deep and full. Spend time discussing the silence and the quality of feelings that you felt. Share the message of the beam of light.

# 28

# Relaxation or Sleep

## Guide: Madeleine Cooper, M.S.W.

*"Watch the clouds and drift into a
special place of well-being and peace."*

## Introduction

The reliving in my mind of a personal retreat to the mountains of New Mexico created such a sense of peace and well-being that I was moved to create this journey in order to share that feeling with others. It is simple and easy to identify with. I have created tapes for my clients to use at them, and they report regular use with excellent results. It is particularly good for those new to guided imagery.

## The Journey

Settle down comfortably in your chair; feet flat on the floor, or if you are using this as a sleep meditation, snuggle into your bed. Pull the covers up if you wish. Let yourself relax. When you are comfortable you will start your special breathing. Breathe in the energy through your nose and exhale through your mouth... in with the fresh air and energy. As you exhale all the tensions start to leave you... relax... in through your nose... exhale feeling the tension leave you... in... out... continue your special breathing.... Your face feels relaxed.... Your shoulders are relaxed.... The muscles of your back are relaxed.... You let all the tensions go.... Your whole body is relaxed.... Just let it happen. Now let your breathing return to its natural rhythm. You find each time you practice relaxation, it will come more and more quickly, more and more deeply as tension slips away. Let the relaxation take over.

To deepen this relaxation, imagine yourself on a mountain path. The air is clean and fresh. It is late afternoon in the summer. The pine trees stand tall and stately to your right. You hear the rustle of aspen to your left. Your eye catches the shimmering of the leaves in the soft breeze. The path slopes downward. It has been cleared—pine needles brushed to the side. You are sure-footed and secure as you walk the earthen path leading in the direction of a meadow ahead. As you reach the edge of the line of trees, you see a hammock between two pine trees. You get into the hammock easily and rock gently. One finger trails the ground making an arc of leaves and pine needles and miniature pebbles. The hammock has a rough texture, but it is comfortable and very safe.

You can see the meadow below you with its carpet of wild flowers spread out... blue, red, white, coral, splashes of green... sunlit... bees humming... a dragonfly flits by.

You look up through the canopy of trees and see a blue sky with high white clouds going by. It is serene, beautiful, peaceful.... You gently rock in the hammock inhaling the energy, the life force and exhaling all tensions... all concerns. The air, rustling leaves, the drifting clouds, the scent of pine, the rough texture of the hammock all bring a special calm... sense of peace... a sense of inner nourishment.

An owl flies by and lights on a branch above you. It doesn't frighten you. Rather you feel a sense of curiosity. You continue to lie there in your hammock looking at the owl. The owl is looking at you. It ruffles its feathers before settling comfortably.... Something passes between you... some unspoken communication.... You have a feeling of inner confidence. Your feeling of relaxation is deeper. Allow yourself the time to relax.

The owl flies away. You watch the clouds drifting in large white puffs pushing one another more rapidly than before.... It is misting.... The soft touch of moist air is on your cheeks. You stop rocking and touch the dampness on your face. You know it's going to rain. You can already hear the first drops falling on the leaves nearby. You leave your hammock and start walking up the mountain path.

If you are using this as a sleep meditation, you will continue to sleep, then wake up relaxed and refreshed at the time you choose. If this is not a sleep meditation you come back to your waking state knowing you can return to your special place whenever you wish. It is a place where you can stretch out on your hammock and watch the clouds drift by... a place where rest and peace and inner healing take place.

You go up the path and with five steps now, you are more and more wide awake and aware of your surroundings. One up the hill, two feeling better than ever before, coming awake, bringing a sense of relaxation and peace, three feeling refreshed — as though you have had a refreshing, invigorating nap, four energizing, five eyes open... alert... wide awake... stretch... smile.... Have a wonderful day.

*Madeleine Cooper, M.S.W. is the clinical director of the Mojave Mental Health Clinic in Las Vegas, Nevada.*

# 29

# Rest Well

## Guide: Geneva B. Mitchell, D.C.H.

*"Create a feeling of peace, freedom, love, comfort, and power over yourself."*

## Introduction

In "Resting Well," you must remember that you are in charge. Know the power that you have within; feel this wonderful power and use it. It is yours. You have the power to do with your life what you will.

## The Journey

Close your eyes. See yourself as you desire to be. Just imagine a clear golden glowing light surrounding your body. Keep the light around you as we begin our journey together. We are going to stretch and be. So when you are ready let's begin.

It's a clear, beautiful July morning. You are on an island. The island is anywhere you desire and anyone or no one is along. Look up into the sky; notice a few thin clouds and hear and finally locate seagulls drifting and swooping, their every movement is easy and slow. You move easy and slow. Then you may decide to not move and just be. You find a shady spot on a sloping hill that overlooks the ocean and lean back, close your eyes and drift, dream or sleep. Hear my voice, the seagulls or not. It's not important. All is well and wonders are all around you. And golden light surrounds all of you. Freedom feels free. You are freedom. So, with your eyes closed and feeling light or heavy, you dream beautiful dreams of interesting events and places. Dream of a house with grassy sloping lawns, wide porches around water, a stream in front of the house, children playing, laughter, fun, running games.

**Pause**

Enter the house, feel at home, find your place. Relax. Go into the deepest part of you and see sincerity, freedom, intelligence, pure joy and talent. See and feel a new level of communication with all those involved in your life. A new awareness of control over all and every part of your life, freedom from anxiety, stress, control. Allowing others the same freedom and control, drift, down, down, down, feel nothing, hear only selected phrases.

**Pause**

Feel only love, conscious of none or all of the above. On the way to all of your goals, dreams and desires, you are aware of all that is of importance. Free from useless baggage, emotions and feeling; powerless findings gone. Strong feelings get stronger, more powerful than ever before, knowing of abilities beyond imaginings or expectations. Breathe in positive power. Breathe it all in finally so-o-o-o good now — go deeper — sleep and rest — So-o-o good, let go and be.

**Pause**

The sea sings to you so you're there or here or anywhere and it's O.K. There is no time here so it's O.K to drift deeper and rest. All organs rest, heart rhythm good, blood flows good. Muscles, nerves, brain, spinal cord, and vertebrae in line. Now freedom, perfection go on into sleep. Set your time to awaken, it's O.K. You're being served by the master within this wonderful creation, you. Only you say when you return and you may choose soon. When you do, if you do, count to 3. Slowly or sleep. All is good, very good. All is fine. Very fine. Free.

*Geneva B. Mitchell is founder and director of New Image Hypnosis Center in Albuquerque, New Mexico. She is a dedicated, motivated hypnotherapist with many interests such as writing and public speaking. She has recently published two books,* Take The Power *and* This Life is Yours.

# 30

# Sensory Soother

## Guide: Edie Weinstein-Moser, M.S.W.

*"Float on a cloud without effort."*

## Introduction

So many people who have sought my assistance have been looking for an effective means of reducing psychological stress and the accompanying physical tension. The areas of the body that manifest the stress are primarily the head, neck, shoulders, and back. We carry so many burdens in our minds that it often literally feels as if we are carrying a sack of rocks. "Sensory Soother" allows you to unburden yourself by focusing not on the pain but on the other functions of the body — namely the senses. Smiles of relief and sighs of serenity seem to indicate that many people are able to let go of some of the burdens. The clients who have used this exercise have experienced a profound sense of deep relaxation as if floating on a cloud, free of any effort on their part.

## The Journey

Allow yourself to begin by drawing in one... full... deep and easy breath. As the air flows into your body, imagine that it contains soothing properties. Each portion of your body that it touches, can only relax... then when you release the breath, the air that flows from your body carries the tension that you may have been feeling when you began. Let it go... see it moving from your body. When you bring in the next breath, feel it moving to an even deeper place within you, soothing and relaxing even more of your body and bringing up even more tension, even more toxins, releasing even more tightness... You may need to consciously think about each breath you take, but soon it will come very naturally.

### Pause

Just for a moment, be aware of any place in your body that feels uncomfortable. Say the word to yourself, like "head" or "neck" or "foot." Then, as you take your next breath, send the air to those parts of your body, allowing them to relax. See in that vivid imagination of yours, your toes uncurling, knots untying or any stiffness being soothed, like wrinkles being ironed out of a shirt. Ah... That's it... Now that you are relaxing more and more deeply in your body, feel growing sense of ease moving into your mind, just like a fine mist... See the mist in any color that you find soothing. Continue to breath it in and watch it curl around your thoughts, gently embracing them and reminding them that this is your time to be at peace, to be at ease, regardless of whatever is happening in your life. All that is real is the here and now, so let it be....

### Pause

If troubling thoughts arise, that's all right... Let them be and send the mist to surround them. Watch what happens when you do that... Good... Now that you are moving deeper and deeper into peace and ease, imagine that you are standing in a beautiful place. Because this is your time, you may choose any place that gives you the feeling of tranquility. It may be somewhere you have visited or somewhere you have always wanted to go... It's up to you. Drink in this place with all of your senses keenly attuned. See the colors... shapes... designs.

**Pause**

Hear the sounds of music... or voices... or laughter... perhaps there are birds or animals around you.

**Pause**

Draw in a breath and smell something delightful... the sense of smell evokes powerful memories for us, so choose a smell that reminds you of something pleasant and soothing.

**Pause**

Reach out and touch the objects or people or creatures around you gently, curiously as if for the very first time.... Perhaps you feel a breeze caressing your skin... or ruffling your hair... or the sun gently glowing on your face.

**Pause**

Is there something to taste... maybe a cool refreshing tropical fruit flavored beverage... or a rich creamy piece of chocolate... Savor the flavor of what you find there.

**Pause**

Now that your senses are feeling fully alive, check in with

your thoughts and feelings and bodily sensations. What is happening within you? Take a few more moments to immerse yourself in this experience.

**Pause**

Now take one last... long look around you, knowing that you may return anytime you choose. This is your place and will always belong to you... but for now, it is time to return to this room... this time... this place... Take another deep breath and ever so slowly, become aware of the sensation of what is supporting you, anything you are experiencing with those finely tuned senses of yours and when you are ready, gently open your eyes, moving and stretching as you need to... Welcome back.

*Edie Weinstein-Moser, M.S.W., is co-publisher of* Visions Magazine *in Miami, Florida. The publication focuses on psychology, health, fitness, the environment, as well as peace, and social justice issues. She also works with individuals and groups in facilitating personal growth.*

# 31

# Thumb and Finger

Guide: William J. Ronan, M.S.

*"A simple way to deal with the day-to-day stresses of life."*

## Introduction

This technique was developed to assist people in dealing with immediate stress that accompanies withdrawal from drugs. I later discovered that it is also an excellent method for helping anyone reduce daily stresses. It has the added feature of being compact and efficient.

## The Journey

Let yourself relax and go to your special place.

If you would like to be able to access this state in stressful situations, try the following:

Imagine a stressful situation such as asking for a raise, giving a speech, or whatever situation you choose. Once you have some of the feelings associated with that anxiety, then place the thumb and finger together gently.

Feel the tension leave your body. Let it go as if it is draining out the tips of your fingers. Then let yourself return to your deeply relaxed state in your special place.

Repeat this technique several times, and you will find it becomes a conditioned response. Eventually the stressful situation can elicit the relaxation response automatically.

*William J. Ronan, L.I.C.S.W., is a medical hypnoanalyst and clinical member of the American Academy of Medical Hypnoanalysts and a full member of the Minnesota Society of Hypnosis in Minneapolis. He provides psychotherapy and education at Applied Behavioral-Health Care*

# 32

# Window

## Guide: Larry Moen

*"Creating a window in your mind's eye
allows new visions and insight."*

### Introduction

This meditation allows you to delve into a deeper personal
dimension and experience the richness of your own inner
being. Doors and windows are symbols of opportunity, and
the use of such imageries deepens your abilities to see beyond
the limited scope of every day thinking.

### The Journey

Close your eyes and take a deep breath. Exhale slowly, letting
all of your muscles, from your scalp to your toes, relax
completely. Inhale again, and slowly exhale, releasing any
remaining tension in your body. As you continue to breathe
deeply and steadily, let your mind relax and drift gently until
you find yourself standing on a white sand path.

The path is smooth and firm beneath your feet. You begin to
move forward. A lush tropical forest is spread on either side
of the path. It is cool and shady, yet light with dappled
sunshine. The white sand path ahead of you is patterned

with sparkling sunlight. On your right, wild hyacinths bloom in warm colors of coral, peach, and fuchsia. You inhale their fragrance. Water drips from the tips of leaves, catching the sunlight as it shines through the forest.

As you continue to walk along the path, you come to a tall tree with a door in its gnarled trunk. Beside the door is a window surrounded by brown bark and shaded by large green leaves.

As you look through the window you find a new world unfolding before your eyes. Notice the colors, the light, the forms you can see. These new visions amaze you, and as you stand gazing joyfully you are aware of your inner strength and peace. You begin to understand, to feel at home, to feel safe....

Now it's time to enter through the door to your Higher Self. Go through it feeling happy and harmonious, open to fully experience this beautiful land. Take time to explore, to enjoy, to be one with your Higher Self....

It is time to leave now. Return from the door and start back along the white sand path. You move beyond the fragrant flowers, the path still smooth and firm beneath your feet. As you walk you hear the slight rustle of the trees. The lush tropical forest is now a part of you. You feel one with all living things. You become more awake, more energetic. Feel your body again, heavy and relaxed. Breathe deeply, letting the breath revitalize your body. Slowly curl and release your fingers and your toes. Gently stretch and release every muscle in your body, waking each one individually.

Take a deep breath, exhale, and when you are ready... open your eyes.

# Freedom & Awareness

# 33

# Body Breathing

## Guide: Larry Moen

*"Breathing in synchronization with another is the ultimate in physical oneness."*

## Introduction

"Body Breathing" can be practiced at any time, with your eyes opened or closed. It can be done while you are walking, talking, bathing, washing dishes, waiting for an appointment, or stopped at a traffic light. It is easy to do, feels really good, and creates an inner awareness and calmness that can stay with you for hours. It also brings forth a euphoria of relaxation and physical sensations not often experienced in our daily lives.

## The Journey

Inhale deeply, beginning at your feet, and breathe in through every pore of your body, all the way up to the top of your head. Feel relaxed throughout your entire body as you breathe out through each pore right down to your toes. This is called "body breathing." Breathe in again feeling heavier and deeper. Feel your body with each breath. You are becoming heavier and more relaxed with each inhalation and exhalation. It's important to be aware of your breathing throughout this entire journey because the breathing is the journey.

Find yourself standing on top of a hill in some grass that's about a foot high. Lie down in the tall, deep green grass. As you descend to the ground, you notice the grass creates an opening that separates to make room for your body. Lie flat on your back. Notice the grass all around you begins to weep forward and covers you. You are totally submerged in this grass. It's as soft as silk on your body. Take this time now just to body breathe.

### Pause

You notice there is a figure standing at your feet. It's a figure of a person. This person wants to join you, and you allow him or her into your heart. The grass reopens and accepts this person who kneels down beside you. You spread your arms far apart, welcoming and caressing this person. The grass then covers both of you like a blanket.

Both breathing simultaneously, you inhale through every pore of your body. As you inhale, you feel a wave coming up through your pores from your feet. This wave begins to flow up through your body to your head and then descends back down again when you start your exhalation. The breath weaves between your bodies, going through every pore on the way down. Inhale again, through every pore, feeling a tingling sensation over the entire length of your beautiful body. From the top of your head, down through your neck, your shoulders, your arms, every pore, your chest, your abdomen, your hips, your legs, your feet. When the wave reaches your feet, you begin your inhalation, and the wave comes back again as you feel the breath through every pore, coming upward through your entire body. You notice the person next to you is in sync with you. You are both inhaling each other through your pores. The two of you become one. The wave of breath, comes up through both of your bodies at the same time, the same wave, up to the head. On the exhalation, the wave descends down though both of your bodies at the same time. You become united in a loving way, in a forgiving way. Anything that has happened between the two of you in the past has been released. It is of no concern. You're starting over now. As of right now you are in the present and this is the only time of existence that matters. The importance of life is right here, right now as you both breathe together through every pore of your bodies. You are in love, you are accepting and forgiving. The two of you lie quietly just breathing.

**Pause**

It is time to bid your friend good-bye knowing that both of you will meet again whenever you wish. As the figure fades away, you stretch and smile.

When you are ready you may open your eyes and continue breathing through every pore of your body.

*Larry Moen is the editor and driving force behind the* Meditations *series. As a Vietnam veteran, Mr. Moen has been aware that significant emotional events can influence one's life. Mr. Moen discovered that past programming from childhood forward can be healed and transformed using the powers of guided meditation. Subsequently, Mr. Moen embarked on an intensive study of guided visualization which he incorporates in his work with T'ai Chi, yoga and self-hypnosis. He currently leads meditation groups and speaks at seminars.*

# 34

# Eating in a Sacred Manner

## Guide: Stephen Levine

*"To eat in a sacred manner
we need to learn to eat from the heart."*

### Introduction

To eat in a sacred manner is to be conscious of the interconnected nature of the eaten and the eater. To honor the eaten. To be aware of what the exceptional teacher Thich Nhat Hanh refers to as "interbeing."

To eat in a sacred manner we need to learn to eat from the heart. Thus we begin with the soft-belly meditation, which allows us to loosen the long-held grief that tightens the belly. Touching with mercy and awareness the pain that imprisons the stomach deep in hard belly, we free the stomach to take nourishment at last. And we attend to each element of this sacred process.

When we eat in a sacred manner, the body is fed for survival and service. Eating doesn't stop at the tongue. We offer sustenance to the whole body, received in soft belly. We honor the process of life and the lineage of creatures sacrificed to the plate. We eat for the benefit of all sentient beings....

To eat in a sacred manner is to eat mindful of the sacred, the one life we all share. To eat in a sacred manner is to attend directly to the underlying divinity of all that eats and is eaten.

## The Journey

As you approach the table reflect on the death-defying act of eating.

Sit in your chair and feel the chair beneath the buttocks. Feel its support against the back.

Feel this body sitting there.

Be aware of the body in its relationship to the table and the food on the plate. Body awareness.

Honor the food on the plate. Notice the shapes of the food, its color. Notice how color defines form. How the green curve of a pea against the white plat delineates its roundness. Learning to see how to see.

### Pause

Having examined the food in its present form, envision the food in its original condition. In the bread, golden fields of wheat waving in the wind. Mountain streams. Eggs in a nest. The black and white Guernsey which offered the milk. The green peas nestled in pods of flowing vines. The dark earth. The rain. And always the sun. Rice paddies. Bean stalks. Potatoes dug by strong hands from the ground.

And if there is meat on the plate, see the animal from which it came. The cows in the field, or in trucks shipped to market. The herds of docile sheep. The snorting swine. The silent fish.

Then picture yourself gathering the food — perhaps singing or chanting to the life about to be consumed. See yourself picking the asparagus, selecting tomatoes from the plant, cutting the wheat or grain, sorting herbs or spices. And if there is meat, picture that animal. Sing to her. Praise him. Send gratitude for the flesh offered.

This is an envisioning, with the heart's eye, of the food which is to be consumed.

Honoring the origins of the food, focus on the environment in which the food is to be consumed. The table, the table-cloth, the design on the plate. The levels in the salt and pepper shakers. The slight curve of liquid as it adheres to the edges of the glass.

Bless the food on the plate. See each mouthful as if it were one more breath, allowing life to remain in the body a moment longer. Thank it. Use it well.

Inhale its aroma. Notice how the fragrance of food is de voured in the nostrils. Savor directly the separate aromas Attend to how the aroma of the steaming peas smells differ ently from that of the baked potato. Watch how fragrance stimulates desire. Fragrance is foreplay. Learning to smell.

Observe how desire comes rapidly to the surface from a sideways glance, a momentary sniff, a passing memory.

Inhaling mindfully. Exhaling mindfully

Reaching for a utensil, the muscles in the arm, the extensors and contractors, are experienced directly as they respond to the intention to pick up the fork, the knife, the chopsticks. Honoring the weight of the fork in the hand. Feel its roughness. Its smoothness. Its coldness. Its increasing warmth. Watch these sensations constantly changing. Learning to touch.

Contact directly the sensations arising from the utensil felt in the hand.

Having noticed the intention to pick up the fork, and feeling the fork thoroughly in the hand, in the fingers, attend to the muscles of the forearm and biceps as the fork arcs toward the plate.

Sacred presence in a body at a table.

Feel the tip of the fork angling for food and the slight change in weight as the food is raised from the plate.

Sensations flowing from the plate toward the mouth.

Investigating the cold of the fork as it touches the lips. Feel the jaw swing open to expose the oral cavity to food. Direct touching.

Hearing the fork as it scrapes against the plate, notice too the birds in the trees, the wind in the branches. The noise in the street, the voice in the mind. Learning to hear.

Feel the food on the tongue. Direct sensation.

Notice the intention of the mouth to close.

Tasting the food on the tongue. Honor its various textures and how they change with mastication. Notice the elements of sweetness or sourness, bitterness or spice, that comprise each moment of tasting. Noticing moment to moment the ever-changing quality of flavor. Learning to taste.

Notice any automatic or mechanical quality in the chewing process. Slowing down, tasting thoroughly. Tasting directly.

Honoring the mind's response to the food, notice how automatically liking and disliking arises from bite to bite.

How liking leads to longing.

How longing energizes expectation.

How expectation fears dissatisfaction.

How that fear of "less" propels intention.

How intention crafts response.

How response becomes lost in reaction.

How reacting, we act in the same old way.

See how mindfulness of the sacred stops the conspiracy.

Honoring this ancient momentum, we do not meet it with judgment but with mercy and respect. Watch the chain of events in the mind as passing show.

Notice how each moment conditions the next.

Honoring the process floating in sacred emptiness.

Observe desire's relationship to food. The drive toward gratification. The leaning toward more. Observe directly the mind. Learn to think. Learn to feel.

In each mouthful opportunities for the sacred. For sacred touching. For sacred hearing. For sacred smelling. For sacred thinking. For sacred feeling.

And in the heart such gratitude for this moment of life, this sacred morsel.

*In the mid-1970's, while working with Ram Dass (*Grist for the Mill, *1976) Stephen Levine taught meditation in the California prison system. For the next few years he led workshops and learned from the terminally ill the need for deeper levels of healing and the profound joy of service (*A Gradual Awakening, *1979). In 1979 he began teaching workshops with his wife, Ondrea. As co-directors of the Hanuman Foundation Dying Project, they continue to serve the terminally ill and those deeply affected by loss.*

*For information about workshops with Stephen & Ondrea Levine or tape order information, please contact Warm Rock Tapes, PO Box 108, Chamisal, New Mexico 87521.*

# 35

# Focusing on a Feeling

## Guide: Jacquelyn Small

*"Connect physical feelings with meaning
so emotional wounds can heal."*

### Introduction

This exercise allows you or your clients to become aware of
feelings in the physical body and to connect the feeling with
its meaning, so the emotional wound can heal.

Once the feeling is out, go back and make sure there is only
relief and serenity left. If something else remains that needs
to be dealt with, go for it in the same manner as you did the
first one.

When a feeling is willing to dialogue with its host, you might
find it useful to have it tell its body and its mind what it needs
from them. Often we gain insight when we see how our
different selves are working or not working together. For
example, my emotions once told my mind to quit giving
them so much data to process. My emotions felt they had to
block off a lot of feeling because they couldn't handle all the
thoughts that came in. And my emotions told my body they
wanted to color my body some beautiful colors, because my
body was too devoid of feeling sometimes, too aligned with

my mental life. This insight has helped me greatly in aligning my physical, emotional, and mental selves.

## The Journey

When your client expresses something you sense must have feeling accompanying it, ask her if she is experiencing a feeling somewhere in her body as she talks. If she says no, then just continue to listening to her. If she says yes, have her point to where the feeling is located.

Then ask her to close her eyes and go to the feeling, focusing her entire attention there. Have her watch the feeling to see what happens, reporting to you as she notices changes. Stay with her, following the feeling wherever it wants to go.

### Pause

Often the feeling will dissolve when noticed, and you can share this insight with your client: "It only wanted you to notice it. Now it can go away." Or, sometimes the feeling will become intensified. If so, have her focus on the feeling. Stay with it. If she tries to leave, keep bringing her back.

### Pause

As it intensifies, allow the feeling to speak. *Not* the intellect, the feeling. The feeling has a voice. "Let it talk to you."

### Pause

As the feeling speaks its mind, help your client express the feeling — cry, moan, yell, whatever is asking to be expressed. If there is no emotional release, have your client ask the feeling what it needs in order to let go and then follow the feeling's instructions.

Example: The feeling might say, "I need to be alone with you to experience this." Or, "I need for you to express this directly to your father." Or, "I need permission to express myself."

*Jacquelyn Small, M.S.S.W., author of* Becoming Naturally Therapeutic *and* Awakening in Time, *has touched the lives of thousands in the innovative workshops and lectures she conducts throughout the U.S. and Canada. She currently serves on the advisory board for the National Council on Codependence. Her company, Eupsychia Inc. is a healing and training center dedicated to bridging traditional and transformational psychologies.*

*From* Transformers: The Artists of Self-Creation *by Jacquelyn Small. Copyright © 1982 by Jacquelyn Small. Used by permission of Bantam Books, a division of Bantam Doubleday Dell Publishing Group, Inc.*

# 36

# Morning Meditation

## Guide: Swami Dayananda

*"One has to see the beauty of prayer.*
*There is no meditation, no ritual without prayer."*

## Introduction

There is no technique which can replace prayer because in any technique the will is retained. Here, the will willingly submits. That submission performs the miracle.

Human free will finds its total expression in a quiet voluntary prayer. Therefore, what I feel and say at these prayerful moments is very important. That I can pray is itself a blessing, and how I pray makes prayer meaningful to me.

The past seems to have a tight hold on each of us. To simply let go of one's past is just wishful thinking. It does not just *happen*. If one can have degree of awareness of this problem, one can discover hope and the solutions in a well-directed prayer.

## The Journey

A prayer is always from an individual. It is never from the self, but from the individual who is nothing but the self in fact. It is this individual who prays.

To whom does the individual pray? I do not pray to another individual. Any other individual also has the limitations that I have as an individual. The power and knowledge of the one I pray to are free from any limitation.

Let there be no confusion about whom the individual is praying to. The self? The individual *is* the self. The self is not an individual, but the individual is the self. Therefore the prayer is not towards the self but towards the self as the Lord. The self that is now an individual is praying to the self that is the total, the Lord.

Let there be no confusion about this. A prayer is always to the Lord. Even the enlightened person who know the meaning of the sentence, "That Thou Art," can offer a prayer as an individual because the difference between the Lord and the individual is evident, even though there is no difference in fact.

Nondifference between the Lord and the individual is a matter for knowledge. That the difference is apparent must be recognized. But, now, as an individual, when I see myself helpless, I cannot but pray. So, prayer is not against the teaching. In fact, any form of ritual, also a kind of prayer, is not against the teaching. I pray because I seek help. Therefore, the prayer is never to the laws themselves but to the laws as the Lord. Therefore, the prayer is always to the Lord, the maker of the world and its laws. Even a prayer directed to a deity, with reference to a given phenomenon like sun, water, fire, and so on, goes to the Lord.

I seek help in order to accept my past. The past is not a villain, nor does it have to be looked upon with contempt. The past makes me what I am. Every experience was an enriching experience. The problem is not that I have a past, but that I see myself as a victim of the past because I do not accept it. Let this be clear. I do not hate my past.

In such hatred there is denial of the past, rejection of the past. I cannot deny my past, much less reject it. The past has happened. It is an already established fact. I cannot do anything to alter the fact. The problem is that when I reject the past, when I resent anything about the past, I do not accept the past. When I criticize myself, I criticize the past. This means I do not accept the past. The more I am able to see how the past cannot change, the more I become free of my resentments, anger, remorse, and so on.

We spend our time and energy resenting the past. I seek help here because it is one thing to understand the past but quite another to be free from resentment and anger towards it. Prayer does something because there is submission. Prayer itself is an action, and its result is called grace. I create the grace. I do not wait for grace to come to me. I invoke it by prayer. That I pray also produces a result because there is an acknowledgment of my own helplessness in the submission.

If I understand how I cannot change my past, why am I angry? Why do I hate myself? Why do I criticize myself? Well, I am helpless. In that acknowledgment of helplessness and in the capacity to pray is my effort, my will. My will is used prudently in submitting. In submission, it is the will that is submitted, and to submit my will, I use my will.

One has to see the beauty of prayer. There is no meditation, no ritual, without prayer. There is no technique which can replace prayer because in any technique the will is retained. Here, the will willingly submits. That submission performs the miracle. In the submission itself, there is an acceptance. Understand that in the submission there is acceptance of the past.

I do not change the self-criticizing mind. I do not want a mind that will not criticize me or anyone else. That is not the issue for me. All that I want is to accept that mind. Let me accept the self-criticizing mind. When I say I accept my past, then I accept the outcome of the past. The outcome is self-criticism. I accept the mind as it is. I am not afraid of this self-judging mind, this self-condemning mind. All that I seek is to totally accept this self-criticizing mind.

O, Lord, help me accept the mind, the self-judging, self-criticizing, self-condemning, self-pitying mind, me. Please help me. I submit my will because I have tried to use my will to change. It did not work. It will never work. And therefore I give up. I give up not helplessly. I give up prudently and deliver myself, my will, into your hands. I have no reason for despair. All I seek is this acceptance of the past with its outcome. I am not avoiding self-criticism. I do not want your grace to stop self-criticism. I want your grace to accept self-criticism.

*Swami Dayananda Saraswati has been teaching Vedanta in India for the past thirty years, and since 1976 he has given lecture tours at many universities in the United States. In 1982, Swami Dayananda established Arsha Vidya Gurukulam as an institute for the traditional teaching of Vedanta and Sanskrit in the West. For more information or to request a catalog of books and tapes, please contact Arsha Vidya Gurukulam, P.O. box 1059, Saylorsburg, PA 18353.*

# Inner Guides

# 37

# In The Sanctuary

## Guide: Rev. Ernestine W. Cline

*"Draw healing energy into your body, mind, and spirit."*

### Introduction

This journey was created to aid one in the centering and focusing of energy. It clears and cleanses the aura. It is an effective exercise for assisting one in gaining greater awareness of his/her own inner soul experience. As one continues to use this journey the intuitive processes become more sensitized and active. One becomes more attuned to his or her higher purpose. With continued practice, this visualization creates a healing experience and the individual can find his or her whole life more enriched and fulfilled. Healing occurs at the physical, mental-emotional, and spiritual levels.

### The Journey

Sit upright, comfortably with both feet on the floor. Breathe slowly and deeply, allowing your body to gently relax. Now, begin to see your breath as pure light. Breathe it into your body allowing the light to move into every cell of your body. See your physical form filled with radiant light. Now, with each breath, allow the light to expand beyond your physical form until it fills your entire energy field. See yourself in your sphere of energy. Know that you are a sphere of radiant, dazzling light. Hold that image and breathe deeply allowing that light to intensify and expand. Feel the peace and contentment that surrounds you.

Now, draw your awareness into your sphere of energy. Bring it to the center point of your sphere, wherever you feel that to be.

**Pause**

Now, find yourself in the sacred sanctuary of the inner temple. Feel the quiet peace that you find here. Know that you may come to this place anytime your choose.

Observe the surroundings. In silence, you sit in this healing place. Begin to enjoy all that you find there. A flowing fountain feeds a gentle stream of water that flows softly close by you. Listen to the music of the rippling waters, the whisper of the wings of a butterfly. Or, create your surroundings as you wish.

**Pause**

Now you become aware of an altar. You approach the altar and become aware of the blue flame that burns upon it. Kneel at the altar and place all of your cares and concerns in the blue flame of divine will and purpose. Release them and let them go. Allow your cares to be consumed in the blue flame of divine will. Sit now, for awhile in the silence. Listen only to the voice of wisdom and truth.

## Pause

With your heart filled with freedom and thanksgiving you return to the center of your inner sanctuary.

Once again begin to be aware of your breath. Breathe slowly and deeply. Take all the time you need to move your awareness comfortably back to your physical world. Gently stretch your body and move only when you are aware and ready. So be it!

*Ernestine Wolfe-Cline, who resides in Fort Myers, Florida, is a minister, artist, teacher who uses her intuitive and artistic abilities to assist others in their search for greater awareness and spiritual direction in their lives. She has developed a meditative process for creating artworks and teaching others to express their own creativity through drawing and paintings. Her artworks are found in most of the fifty United States and eleven foreign countries.*

# 38

# Meeting an Inner Adviser

## Guide: David E. Bresler, Ph.D.

*"Communication with your adviser fosters a 'centering process,' in which your ability to observe your intuitive side becomes very sophisticated."*

### Introduction

This technique — perhaps the most fascinating form of guided imagery — allows patients to communicate actively with the non-dominant part of their brain, and in turn reach a more complete understanding of their pain experience.

The advisers that people create using this imagery are able to reach the inner recesses of the unconscious mind. The adviser can also help change unconscious belief systems.... Your adviser can keep you intimately connected with your unconscious mind and can tell you how well you are incorporating, new beliefs, new expectations, and new habits.

There's no better place to seek out your adviser than in the calm, peaceful, personal place that you have previously discovered.

### The Journey

Before beginning, take a moment to get comfortable and relaxed. Sit upright in a comfortable chair, feet flat on the floor, and loosen any tight clothing or jewelry or shoes that might distract you. Make sure you won't be interrupted for a few minutes. Take the telephone off the hook, if necessary...

Now, take a few slow, deep, abdominal breaths... Inhale... Exhale... Inhale... Exhale... Focus your attention on your breathing throughout this exercise and recognize how easily slow deep breathing alone can help to produce a nice state of deep, gentle relaxation... Let your body breathe itself according to its own natural rhythm, slowly, easily and deeply.

Now let's begin the exercise with the signal breath, a special message that tells the body you are ready to enter a nice state of deep relaxation... Exhale... Breathe in deeply through your nose.., and blow out through your mouth... You may notice a kind of tingling sensation as you take the signal breath. Whatever you feel is your body's way of acknowledging the developing experience of relaxation, comfort, and peace of mind.

Remember your breathing... slowly and deeply. As you concentrate your attention on your breathing, imagine a ball of pure energy or white light that starts at your lower abdomen ,and as you inhale, it rises up the front of your body to your forehead... As you exhale, it moves down your spine, down your legs, and into the ground.

Again, imagine this ball of pure energy or white light rise up the front of your body to your forehead as you inhale... And as you exhale, it moves down your spine, down your legs, and into the ground... Circulate the ball of energy around for a few moments... Allow its circulation to move you into even deeper states of relaxation and comfort...

Each time you inhale and exhale, you may find yourself twice as relaxed as you were a moment before... Twice as comfortable... Twice as peaceful... For with each breath, every cell of your body becomes at ease... Let go, as all the tension, tightness, pain, or discomfort drains down your spine, down your legs and into the ground... Continue to circulate this ball of energy around for a few moments...

Remember your breathing, slowly and deeply from the abdomen... Now take a brief inventory of your body, starting at the top of your head working down to the tips of your toes... Is every part of your body totally relaxed and comfortable? If so, enjoy how it feels. However, if there is still any part of your body that is not yet fully relaxed and comfortable, simply inhale a deep breath now and send it into that region, bringing soothing, relaxing, nourishing, healing oxygen into every cell of that area, comforting it and relaxing it. As you exhale, imagine blowing out through your skin any tension, tightness, pain or discomfort from that area.

Again, as you inhale, bring relaxing healing oxygen into every cell of that region, and as you exhale blow away through the skin and out into the air any tension or discomfort that remains in that area... In this way, you can use your breath to relax any part of your body that is not yet as fully relaxed and comfortable as it can be... Breathe slowly and deeply, and with each breath, you may find that you have become twice as relaxed as you were before, and that you are able to blow away twice as much tension and discomfort as you did with the previous breath... Inhale... Exhale... Twice as relaxed... Inhale... Exhale... Twice as comfortable.

As you allow yourself to enjoy this nice state of deep, peaceful relaxation, think of your favorite place, a place that's beautiful, peaceful, serene and secure. A magical, special place just for you.

Let your imagination become reacquainted with every detail of this beautiful spot... Sense the peacefulness all around you... Stretch out... Relax... And enjoy it.

As you relax in your favorite spot, put a smile on your face... and slowly look around. Somewhere, nearby, some living creature is waiting for you... Smiling and waiting for you to establish eye contact... This creature may immediately approach you or it may wait a few moments to be sure that you mean it no harm...

Be sure to look up in the trees or behind bushes, since your adviser may be a bit timid at first... But even if you see nothing, sense his or her presence and introduce yourself... Tell your adviser your name, and that you mean no harm, for you've come with only the friendliest intentions.

Find out your adviser's name... The first name that comes to your mind... Right now. Any name...

Put some food out before you... And ask your adviser if he or she is willing to come over and talk with you for a few moments... Don't be alarmed if your adviser becomes quite excited and starts jumping up and down at this point... Often, advisers have been waiting a long time to make this kind of contact... Until now, your adviser has only been able to talk to you sporadically through your intuition... Tell your adviser you're sorry you haven't listened more in the past, but that you'll try to do better in the future...

If you feel silly talking in this way, tell your adviser that you feel silly... That it's hard for you to take this seriously... But if you sincerely want your adviser's help, make that very, very clear... Tell your adviser that you understand that like in any friendship, it takes time for feelings of mutual trust and respect to develop...

Although your adviser knows everything about you — since your adviser is just a reflection of your inner life — tell your adviser that you won't push for any simple answers to important questions that you may be dealing with... Rather, you'd like to establish a continuing dialogue... So that anytime you need help with a problem, your adviser can tell you things of great importance... things that you may know, but you may know their significance...

If there's a problem that's been bothering you for a while, ask your adviser if he or she is willing to give you some help with it... Yes or no... Your adviser's response is the first answer that pops into your mind... Pose your questions as you exhale... And the first response that comes into your mind as you inhale is your adviser's reply... It's an inspiration... Ask your questions now.

**Pause**

What did your adviser reply?... Ask any other questions that are on your mind...

**Pause**

Continue this dialogue for a few moments... Asking your questions as you exhale... And listening to the response that pops into your mind as you inhale...

### Pause

Remember, your adviser knows everything about you, but sometimes — for a very good reason — he or she will be unwilling to tell you something... This is usually to protect you from information you may not be ready to deal with... When this occurs, ask your adviser what you need to do in order to make this information available to you... Your adviser will usually show you the way...

If there is something that you'd like your adviser to be thinking about between now and the next time you meet, tell this to your adviser now...

### Pause

If there is anything your adviser would like *YOU* to think about between now and the next time you meet, find out what that is...

### Pause

Set up a time to meet again... A time that's convenient for you and a time that's convenient for your adviser... Be specific as to exact time and place... Tell your adviser that although these meetings are important to you, part of you is lazy or reluctant to follow through...

One way your adviser can help motivate you to continue meeting periodically is by giving you a clear demonstration of the benefits you can gain... A demonstration so powerful that you will be moved to work even harder in getting to know yourself... If you are in pain, for example, ask your adviser if he or she is willing to help motivate you by taking away that pain completely... Right now, just for a few moments, as a demonstration of power... If so, tell your adviser to do it... now...

Notice any difference?... If you're willing to do your share of the work, by relaxing yourself and meeting periodically to set things straight, there's no limit to your adviser's power... Ask for any reasonable demonstration that will undeniably convince to you of this power...

You might be, for example, somewhat forgetful... And although you want to continue these meetings with your adviser, you might forget the exact time and place that you agreed to meet... If so, ask your adviser to help you by coming into your consciousness just a few moments before it's time to meet, to remind you of the meeting.

Before leaving, tell your adviser you're open to having many different kinds of advisers... And that you will leave this totally up to your adviser's discretion... If your adviser wants to bring other advisers along the next time you meet, fine... Is there anything your adviser would like you to bring along with you the next time you meet?... If so, find out what that is...

**Pause**

See if your adviser will allow you to establish physical contact... This is very important... Just about every animal on the face of the earth loves to have its face stroked and its back scratched... See if your adviser will allow you to make this contact now...

**Pause**

While making this contact, find out if there's anything else that your adviser would like to tell you... If so, what is it?...

**Pause**

Is there anything that you would like to tell your adviser before you leave?... If so, do it now...

When you are ready, take the signal breath to return from this meeting... But before you do, tell yourself that each time you make contact with your adviser the communication will flow more and more smoothly... More and more easily... More and more comfortably... Tell yourself that when this experience is over, you will feel relaxed, rested, and comfortable, as well as energized with such a powerful sense of wellbeing that you will be able to respond easily to any demands that arise. To end this exercise, simply open your eyes and take the signal breath... Exhale... Inhale... Breathe in deeply through your nose... Blow out through your mouth... And be well.

*David E. Bresler, Ph.D., former Director of the UCLA Pain Control Unit and former professor in the UCLA Medical and Dental Schools and the UCLA Psychology Department, is currently in private practice in Santa Monica, California. He is the executive director of the Bresler Center Medical Group.*

*Reprinted by permission of David E. Bresler, Ph.D. from* Free Yourself From Pain, *P.O. Box 967, Pacific Palisades, CA 90272.*

# 39

# Safe Place

## Guide: Pamela M. Fox, M.S.

*"Safety can be internalized despite the chaos
in the environment around you. "*

**Introduction**

The "Safe Place" journey was created for use with clients
who have suffered from lack of emotional support from
family systems, lack of spiritual trust to the extreme of
physical, sexual, and emotional abuse. As I worked with
individuals who were recovering from various addictions, I
noticed that most of these people were currently living in
situations that were not conducive to safety and support.
Once they left my office, they did not feel protected enough
to take risks that could help them create different lifestyles.

This journey was used in guided meditation in sessions
creating as much detail as possible so the client could easily
recreate this environment wherever he or she may be and
particularly for times of stress. Initially it is best practiced
with your favorite music in a quiet place. After developing
the scene, it may help to actually draw what you see. In time,
it will become as easy as five deep breaths to bring about the
safety and security you need to meet whatever challenge
comes your way.

## The Journey

Begin by relaxing into an even breath, in and out of your body, releasing tension as you exhale. Allow yourself to do this several times.

Imagine yourself walking down a long path. As you walk down this path, look around you and notice the trees. Can you smell any fragrance? How does the ground feel under your feet? Pick up some leaves, needles, pine cones, stones, or whatever you find as you're walking. Take a long, slow, deep breath, smell the air and notice whether the air is cold or warm as it is entering your nose, throat and lungs.

After a while you come to a clearing — look around — notice if there is a structure. Is it a building, cabin, cave or any other natural structure? Look for openings as you begin to investigate this safe place. Again use all of your senses to create this place for yourself.

### Pause

Now slowly enter and begin to look around. Are there any furnishings in this environment? Are there pictures on the wall or any unusual objects? Is there anything familiar here that may allow you to feel safe, secure and connected to your inner guide? Allow your guide to manifest in whatever form it needs to take. If you have any questions at this time — pose them to your guide. Then be silent for a while to allow your answers to come.

### Pause

If there are no answers at this time, just be aware over the next few days for responses in the form of people, books or thoughts.

Now gently bring your awareness back to your breathing and begin to come back down the path. Hear the sounds around you and slowly allow your consciousness to be brought to your current reality. Remember you can go to this place any time you need to be centered.

*Pamela M. Fox, M.S., is a psychotherapist in private practice Naples, Florida. She was formerly director of patient treatment of eating disorders at the Willough of Naples. She is a licensed mental health counselor who works with all kinds of clients who want to uncover the reasons that their lives are not as successful as they would like them to be.*

# Gifts & Love

# 40

# Friendship

## Guide: Cayce Brooks

*"A friend is a gift to yourself."*

## Introduction

Sometimes we are unable to have a meeting of hearts and minds on the conscious level. This meditation is to facilitate a meeting on the spiritual level to hopefully heal any distances that exist. When family members can't appreciate different points of view, feeling spiritually linked can preserve the sense of family that we all need.

My friends provide me with an extended spiritual family. They are a gift from my higher power to me. If wealth is measured by how many people love you, then I am rich beyond my wildest dreams.

## The Journey

Ground and center. Rise up from the energy of the Earth Mother. Rise up to the heart chakra. See your heart, a beautiful green flower, closed revolving slowly in space. Your heart light shines through, illuminating the dark empty space in which your heart flower floats, serene, peaceful, in eternal bliss. Secure in your self love, will the outer petals to unfold slowly, gently unfold. As each petal unfolds completely, the tip of each petal begins to glow pink with the knowledge of self love.

**Pause**

Breathe in, breathe out, and feel the armor of daily living peel away with the petals as they fall effortlessly from the heart center. Each petal has a green base with a glowing pink tip. Now you see and feel the flower of your heart fully open and receptive, whirling gently in the space of your mind. It is throwing green and pink light in all directions. As you spin with the flower, you notice small points of light hovering in the distance. They are moving closer and closer. You can feel the love energy of them reaching you, caressing your energy field. They float closer and you realize that they are the heartflowers of all your friends. There are so many, twinkling, spinning slowly toward you. Yes, yes, you think, come closer, there is no danger here, not to you or from you.

They spiral in close enough for you to see their faces. They are your family and friends, and they are thrilled to touch you on the spiritual plane. As you touch energy field with first one then another, healing and forgiveness and light and joy suffuse the atmosphere around all of you. You see your flower float to the center of a circle of dancing, joyous heartflowers. As the energy rises you all spin and dance faster, in and out, around and about. You whirl and spiral in your sacred orbits making up the very essence of life. You see all as the spinning of atoms at the base of the energy chain, the revolving of your life in the lives of others, and the music of planets and stars. You see that they dance to the same sacred song. And the song is composed of all the songs each of you sing. The combined effect is the sound of life.

**Pause**

Breathe in the music... breathe out... and hear your own sacred song. Hear how important your friendship is to the others in your life. Breathe in... breathe out... and honor the importance of other's songs in your own life. See the connection of our dance, honor your part. Feel surrounded by the love of your friends. Reach out and surround them in turn. Drop all those barriers and let your dances flow together. These steps are older than time; you know them by heart. You are the dance, and without you, the dance would be incomplete. Realize that you are important to your friends just as you are. Know that you can accept your family and friends just as they are, without losing anything of yourself. Feel the love and acceptance. Breathe in this feeling... breathe out any walls that may remain. Breathe in the love of self and know that to love and accept others, you must first love and accept yourself. Breathe out... breathe in the power of love... all you need is love, breathe out the fears and doubts. Know that on this spiritual plane everyone can be the best they are meant to be including you.

**Pause**

As the knowing of your own self-worth radiates out from the tips of your heartflower, it joins and becomes fused with the long pink fires that are radiating out from all the other heartflowers. The energy lines connect and dance and connect and dance. As the dance slows down and each heartflower floats serenely in it's own space, you see and feel the rays of light and love that form your connection with everyone else in this circle, in this area, and in this part of the universe. You are at oneness with yourself which makes you at one with all. Breathe deeply pulling the pink light through all your being. Be healed, knowing that as long as you have yourself for a friend, you will never be alone. Know that you deserve your friends and that they deserve a fine and spiritual person like you in their lives. Honor your higher power as it is reflected in your friends. This is the face of the Goddess or God, and it is an honor to see it. Breathe in this knowing. Sit with the image of dozens of pink/green flowers gently whirling in the womb of space, lighting the void with their infinite love.

*Cayce Brooks is a poet, artist, carpenter, and mother. She tries to manifest the Divine Feminine in her life by bringing out the sacred in even the most ordinary. She practices earth magic in the mountains of north Georgia surrounded by the love and support of a wide circle of friends.*

# 41

# Receiving Gratitude

Guide: Marjorie Michael Munly

*"Take the time to acknowledge your
success and contributions."*

## Introduction

My personal experiences in a very demanding service profession (teaching) inspired me to create this journey. I found that I, and many of my co-workers, rarely took the time to acknowledge our many successes in working with children. This journey will enable the user to remember and claim contributions to the lives of others. It has been especially useful to those who make significant contributions but always feel they have not done enough. Use this journey any time you feel the lack of acknowledgment from others or from yourself.

## The Journey

Sit comfortably, or lie down, allowing your whole body the well-deserved opportunity to relax. Take a slow deep comfortable breath in through the nose, then, out through the mouth. Repeat this five times.

**Pause**

Next allow your attention to go to each area of your body beginning with your feet. Feel each bone, muscle and joint become very heavy. Your whole body knows that it can let go of any effort.

Imagine that you are about to embark on an effortless journey to a place where you feel safe, at home and at peace. It can be at the beach, mountains, forest or a place remembered from childhood... perhaps even a home or favorite childhood room. Notice the sounds, smells, charm and unique beauty here. They nourish your senses. You are totally supported and at peace.

Reflect back on your life thus far – that is– bring to the front of your memory those people whose lives you have touched in some way by caring, by supporting, by nurturing, by teaching. One by one a loving, familiar face comes before you, expressing a heart felt thank you for what it is you have given..

## Pause

Notice what it is each person has to say. As each expression of gratitude is given, receive it into your heart and mind as truth.

If at any time you wish to be reminded of what you have given, you may call to mind what you have seen and heard here today.

*Marjorie Michael Munly, who lives in Arlington, Virginia, is an early childhood educator and a pioneer of peace and awareness education in the public schools (for staff and students). She has been a teacher of meditation for twenty years*

# 42

# Rose Pink Bubble

Guide: Karen M. Thomson, Ph.D.

*"We are beings of Light and Love."*

## Introduction

As we have been taught, besides loving God and all others, we must also love ourselves, be good to ourselves, gently nurture ourselves. This meditation is a beautifully loving express on the rose pink Light, symbolizing a high concentration of energy that we call absolute and unconditional love. As the vibrations of the body/mind/spirit are raised through this meditation, our abilities to give and receive love are greatly enhanced.

## The Journey

Completely and totally relax as you begin to breathe slowly and deeply. With every inhalation, know that you're breathing in oxygen, energy, Light, and all that's positive; so breathe in slowly and completely fill the body. As you breathe out, exhale completely, and know that you are letting go of toxins, frustration, anxiety, darkness, and anything you no longer need.

Completely and totally exhale, just as you completely and totally inhale. Keep your concentration on your breathing, as both the inhalation and the exhalation are equally important and equally slow, deep, and complete.

With your eyes closed, take a slow, deep breath, and feel your body relaxing from the top of the head, down your scalp, facial muscles, neck, shoulders, down the arms, and out the fingertips. Continue slowly and deeply breathing...

Again, return your awareness to your body, and feel the deep relaxation moving now from your shoulders down your chest, down your spine, down your stomach area, hips, legs, knees, calves, ankles, feet, and out the toes.

Now see your entire body filled with Light and Peace and all that is positive, and as you inhale, breathe in Light and energy, and feel now an even greater state of relaxation. Check out your body. If there is an area of the body where there is discomfort or dis-ease, focus the Light and the Peaceful, Loving, Healing energy there. See the Light absorbing any pain, discomfort, or darkness.

Again, take a deep breath and see the body filled with and surrounded by a most beautiful, peaceful, and loving Light, which now extends several feet from the body. See the body now as surrounded in a cocoon of rose pink Light. You feel as though you are immersed and bathed in pink Light, and as you breathe in deeply, you inhale — drink in — this beautiful pink Light that is now filling and surrounding your body. You are feeling completely peaceful and relaxed, and have a wonderful sense of well-being. In this rose pink bubble of Light, you have the awareness, the knowing that you are completely loving and totally, unconditionally loved.

Stay in the rose pink bubble as long as you like, and bask, bathe in its Light.

## Pause

When you're ready to come out of it, simply open your eyes. You can recall the sense of deep well-being and relaxation and the feeling of total love at any time simply by remembering this experience in the rose pink bubble.

*From the early '70s through the early '90s, Karen M. Thomson has blended an academic career with her metaphysical work. As a full professor with her Ph.D. in English, she taught literature and composition in the college classroom and was also a college administrator in the university system of Georgia. In 1993, she made a dramatic shift in her career and became a full-time practitioner of various metaphysical and healing arts including psychic readings, spiritual counseling, and healing. She lectures, teaches, writes, and provides private counseling.*

# Creativity & Inspiration

# 43

# Chakra Balancing/ Dreamer

## Guide: Chrystle Clae

*"Our subconscious has all the answers, and
it often shares them with us through our dreams."*

## Introduction

The chakras are unseen, specific energy centers in our physical bodies. Stress and normal life experiences can cause them to become unbalanced. Thought creates energy, and this meditation will allow your energies to become cleansed and aligned. The crystal cave that you visit will encourage productive dreaming, which can help your daily life.

## The Journey

Take a lingering deep breath, filling the bottom of your lungs first. (This means the area near your abdomen will rise filled with air before the completion of your inhale, which is when your chest rises.) Hold that breath for a mental count of six..., then exhale slowly and gently through slightly parted lips. Repeat this breath exercise several times. Make a mental note of any places in your physical body that may be holding onto the tension or pressure of your day. Breathe into those areas and feel the tensions release on your exhale.

## Pause

Imagine in your mind's eye any red object — now imagine a spiral of light in that same red shade. See or feel that red spiral of energy pulsating at the base of your spine. Breathe into it and make it more vivid. Let it remain alive and vibrant as you...

Imagine in your mind's eye any orange object — now imagine a spiral of light in that same orange shade. See or feel that orange spiral of energy pulsating in the reproductive organ area of your spine. Breath into it and make it more vivid. Let the orange remain as you...

Imagine in your mind's eye any yellow object — now imagine a spiral of light in that same yellow shade. See or feel that yellow spiral of energy pulsating in the belly-button area of your spine. Breathe into it and make it more vivid. Let the yellow remain as you...

Imagine in your mind's eye any green object — now imagine a spiral of light in that same green shade. See or feel that green spiral of energy pulsating in the area of your heart. Breathe into it and make it more vivid. Let the green light remain as you...

Imagine in your mind's eye any blue object — now imagine a spiral of light in that same blue shade. See or feel that blue spiral of energy pulsating in the throat chakra area of your spine. Breathe into it and make it more vivid. Let the blue remain as you...

Imagine in your mind's eye any deep red-blue color — now

imagine a spiral of light in that same indigo shade. See or feel that indigo spiral of energy pulsating in the third eye area of your brow. Breathe into it and make it more vivid. Let the indigo remain as you...

Imagine in your mind's eye any violet object — now imagine a spiral of light in that same violet shade. See or feel that violet spiral of energy pulsating at the top, or crown, of your head. Breathe into it and make it more vivid. Let the violet remain.

Now take an imaginary step back and view your spiritual body as the beautiful rainbow that your are... a pulsating rainbow of light that is able to feel a oneness with all life in the universe. Take another slow, deep breath and find yourself in a magical summer woods. It's warm outside, so you have on a bathing suit and can feel the cool earth beneath your bare feet.

You're walking on a cleared, dirt path beneath beautiful, tall trees. You're in shade, except for the few rays of sunshine that filter in through the branches and leaves. There are hills throughout this forest and you can see a few animals scurry about. If you look up in the trees you'll see a few birds of the forest flying from one tree to the other and occasionally touching ground... just beyond your reach.

Continue walking on your path and notice anything in the surroundings that attract you.

**Pause**

Now, if you look off to your right, you will see you're approaching a small cave. Go closer.

Above the opening to the cave, someone has placed the sacred symbol for Om on a woodcarving at the entrance. It's just resting on a rock. You know that this symbol is meant to assure protection and blessings to all who enter this cave.

To the left of the entrance is a small, natural spring flowing into a stream. The spring falls from a place just high enough so that it will act as a shower for you. On the right hand side of the cave's entrance is a clean bench where you see that someone has already placed your bed pillow and a clear quartz crystal.

Go beneath the shower of the spring and realize, as it washes you, that this is sacred and holy water that cleanses your spirit as well as your body. This is a purifying spring — allow it to remove any past spiritual hurts. It will enable you to find forgiveness for any hurts you feel you may have caused others. Let it cleanse your aura, your heart and your mind!

**Pause**

As you leave the spring you find that the water didn't leave you wet at all — only refreshed.

Go to the bench with your pillow and the crystal. Stop as you pick them both up and feel the Earth Mother beneath your feet once more. Close your imaginary eyes and feel the balance within your spirit as the Earth allows you to anchor your emotions and feel secure and grounded by her love.

**Pause**

Purified and grounded you can take your pillow and crystal and enter this special cave. Just inside its entrance, you can feel a soft breeze brush your cheek and hair. This is the breeze of Inspiration which encircles your being like a bubble. Its gift is to send you dreams of inspiration that will include symbols for your Teaching Shield. It will be with you, unseen, every time you sleep and request help or guidance from your dreams.

There is a small chamber off to the right in this cave. This is where you are to place your pillow and crystal. The chamber glows from an ultra-violet flame that has no heat. This flame will cleanse any unwanted energy from your belongings and then charge them with enhanced life and energy to be used as aids for your dream work. The pillow will lull you to sleep and direct you to the higher vibrations of reality in the dreaming state.

The crystal given to you is charged to stimulate your connection to the universe, enabling you to have any information you need to aid you in this incarnation, through your dreams. The stone will also record your dreams for you so that remembering them after you awake will be easy.

With that charging complete, the ultra-violet flame's light reflects from your stone directly to your third eye area. This is an added blessing to stimulate your dreaming experiences.

Take a moment, as you exit this cave, to once more feel the earth beneath your feet grounding and nurturing your spirit. Glance down at the stone in your hand and see if it has remained a quartz crystal, or if the charging process in the caves chamber changed it to a different stone that better suits your vibration and needs. Any stone that remains is perfect for you.

Breathe deeply and open your eyes when you feel ready.

# 44

# Creative Resources

## Guide: Martin Rosenman, Ph.D.

*"Generate ideas and mentally rehearse future events."*

## Introduction

This is a simple and powerful method for helping discover your creative resources. As part of my workshops, participants practice this meditation one or twice, and then receive a copy of the tape for future use. It can be used for experiencing deep relaxation, reducing stress, solving problems creatively, or discovering opportunities.

Some people listen to it several times a week, and they report that it helps many of the above situations. Other just listen when they feel they need it.

## The Journey

Close your eyes and prepare to go into a deep and wonderful state of relaxation. Focus on your breath, and as you inhale and exhale say the number one to yourself each time that you exhale. Allow yourself to become more and more relaxed each time that you say the number one to yourself as you exhale.

## Pause

Picture yourself in a very relaxing setting. Allow yourself to become more and more relaxed as you picture and experience your relaxing setting. Allow yourself to become more and more relaxed as you relax all parts of your body. Now feel a sensation in your right big toe. It can be a warm sensation, a relaxed sensation, a heavy sensation, a tingling sensation, a numb sensation or it can be a combination of these sensations. Let the sensation spread to your next toe, to your middle toe. Continue slowly spreading the sensation throughout the parts of your body, finishing with the parts of your head.

## Pause

When your thoughts turn to the consideration of important decisions and important problems for which you have not yet found a solution, you will find that you will be able to focus and concentrate on these topics more effectively. Even when you are not consciously thinking about the problems you would like to solve, your mind will come up with many potentially useful ideas. Some of these ideas are even likely to catch you by surprise, emerging into your awareness while you are thinking of something else. They may occur during sleep when you dream, when you think of an idea in the middle of the night, or when you have ideas upon awakening. These ideas will be helpful to you, but you will always try to make sure that you have sufficient information on which to base any final decision. You will want to check out these new ideas to make sure that they are practical, just as you would check out information from any other source.

Overall, you will be pleased at how much more clearly and creatively you will be able to think.

Picture yourself doing well in a future situation. See yourself, hear yourself, experience yourself performing at the peak of your abilities. You are focused mentally and other people are responding to your positive energy. Mentally rehearse your success for your specific, future, important occurrence.

Inhale deeply, tense and relax all body parts and open your eyes when you are ready.

*Martin Rosenman is a professor of psychology at Morehouse College and a nationally known expert in creative problem-solving and decision making. Dr. Rosenman has worked extensively with the Center for Disease Control, teaching both managers and scientists creative problem-solving techniques to enhance productivity and discovery. He belongs to numerous professional associations and has been published in professional journals and has presented at professional meetings.*

# Training & Skill

# 45

# Concentration-Retention -Total Recall

## Guide: Richard J. Palmer

*"Improve your abilities to receive, retain,
and recall information."*

### Introduction

I was prompted to create this journey because of the many
inquiries I have received over the years from students and
faculty at our local university. With 5,000 employees and
almost 15,000 students, there is a fairly constant flow of
inquiries and clients needing help with their studies. Using
hypnosis, I have been able to help them in many ways to
improve their abilities to receive, retain, and recall information. This journey has been very successful in helping clients.

When using this journey, first use a standard relaxation
dialogue, and when you feel the client is in the relaxed or
lethargic stage, move into the journey. At this stage, the
subconscious is most receptive to the suggestions in the
journey.

I have found that three sessions will generally give the
average student a potent boost in their learning process.
Occasionally, someone undertaking a difficult course of
study, such as engineering, may elect additional sessions.

## The Journey

Fix your eyes on a spot on the ceiling overhead, just pick out an imaginary spot and stare at the spot without moving a muscle. Now take a deep breath and fill up your lungs, exhale slowly, sleep now. Now a second and even deeper breath, exhale, sleep now and now a third deep breath, exhale, sleep now. Now let your eyelids close. As each muscle and nerve begins to grow loose and limp and lazy all of your cares and tensions fade away. You are relaxing more with each sound you hear, with each easy breath that you take. You are going deeper and deeper into drowsy relaxation.

I am going to count from ten down to one and as I do I want you to picture and imagine that you are walking down a flight of steps. With each number that I count, the quality of your deep relaxation becomes more profound and more intense. When I reach the count of one you will then be aware that you are enjoying a very healthful, very pleasant state of hypnotic relaxation. Number ten we take the first step downward, each muscle and each nerve grows loose and limp and relaxed. Number nine the wave of relaxation spreads all across your body. Number eight you're relaxing more with each easy breath that you take, with each sound that you hear you are going deeper and deeper in drowsy relaxation. Number seven every muscle and every nerve is growing loose and limp and lazy. Number six you're moving down to a new and deeper level of hypnotic relaxation. Number five you are halfway down now.

When I reach the count of one, I will say the words *sleep deeply*, you'll then be aware that you are more deeply relaxed than ever before. Number four each muscle and nerve lets loose, relaxing you're drifting down deeper and deeper,

deeper in sleep. Number three going down deeper in drowsy relaxation. Number two — on the next number now I will give the signal. I'll say the words *sleep deeply*. When I do, you'll then be aware that you are enjoying very profound state of hypnotic relaxation. Number one sleep deeply.

Now relax and go deeper into sleep. As you go deeper into relaxation, you realize that you are a constantly growing and maturing person. You are becoming aware of the strengths and abilities that have developed within you. You feel a sense of confidence in your ability to achieve the goals you have chosen for yourself. You are learning to believe in yourself. You appreciate yourself. You do good and kind things for yourself. You meet each situation as it comes with calm and quiet assurance. You are making contact with the center of wisdom and power within you, which knows what to do and how to do it. Whatever you say, whatever you do is said and done with complete confidence and self assurance. You walk with a spring in your step. Your head is held high. You see the beauty of life around you. People respect you because you respect them and you respect yourself. You have confidence in your own judgement and you are honest and dependable. You move forward from one positive achievement to another.

You're aware that it is possible for a person to concentrate so strongly when reading, studying or working that they become completely unaware of things that happen around them. It is possible for you to concentrate like that from now on. Whenever you wish to concentrate, first get ready for the work that you are going to do. Get your books, your writing materials, the tools with which you are going to work; have them ready for the job to be done. Next look at the clock and decide how long you wish to concentrate and then write the time that you are going to end your concentration on a piece of paper. Write it three times. For example, if you are beginning at seven o'clock in the evening and you decide to study until eleven o'clock in the evening. Write it three times on a piece of paper. Look at it, say it aloud three times. As you say those words, begin to concentrate. Your thoughts start to narrow to the job at hand. Your ears start to become less sensitive to surrounding noises; your eyes are drawn to the work you are about to do. Start working, if the project is reading, start reading, if it is writing, start writing. Whatever the job is, start doing it.

Within the next few minutes your concentration increases until you are oblivious to your surroundings; In the next few minutes the rest of the world seems to fade away so that for you, there exists only the job at hand and you are doing that job. Your concentration rapidly becomes perfect and remains that way until the time that you have stated arrives. Your concentration is continuous, unless there is some real and necessary reason to attend to other things. Your concentration is continuous and perfect from a few minutes after you start working until the time you have set for yourself. Your thoughts are all directed at the job at hand. The outside world is far away. Your concentration is perfect until the time you have set for yourself. The knowledge that you acquire in this concentrated way remains in your conscious memory much longer as you read, study or work in this manner. You find your ability to remember facts, details, principles and theories is tremendously increased. You retain a perfect conscious memory of the material that you acquire in this way. You are also simultaneously developing a new ability to remember things that you had previously forgotten. You are becoming aware of a feeling of personal confidence in your intelligence.

You have confidence in your ability to master your studies. When you read, you read with an absolute concentration, and you easily remember what you read. When you listen, you listen intently, and you remember what your hear. You are confident because you have the ability to do the work, the ability to pay close attention to what is said, the ability to concentrate when you are reading, and the ability to remember what you have heard and read. While you are reviewing, your concentration on your books and notes is absolute. When reading for review it is necessary to read only once. This reading will bring to the upper levels of your mind the studies that you have already mastered. During this time you read rapidly and accurately with full understanding. When you go to the examination you are confident of your ability to write a perfect paper. You know the subject and you know that you know the subject. You are calm and self possessed. As you read the first question, a feeling will begin to develop. That feeling will be that you can easily answer the question correctly or that you are uncertain. After reading the question, if you feel the least bit uncertain, pass that question and go on to the next one. Repeat the process.

You have the knowledge to answer all of the questions correctly. As you read each question you are sending an order down to your subconscious mind. This order is that the direct answer be delivered up to the conscious level, and sometimes this takes a little while. As you are reading the next question, the answer to the first one will be working up to the memory level at the same time that you are sending down orders to the other questions. By the time you have finished reading all the questions you will be fully ready to answer the first one that you missed. Remember, if for any reason the answer seems to be a little slow in being delivered, pass that question and go on to the next one. Your second reading of the question will reinforce the order, and by the time you have finished all of the answers that come easily, the answers to the other questions will be ready for you. Remember that usually the last question counts as much as the first one. Never wait for the answer to a question until you have answered the ones that come easily to you. If the examination is an essay type, the same rule applies. Begin writing, and if you run dry or if you feel uncertain, don't waste time, move to the next question and begin writing. The second time you are back to where you left off, the answer will flow much more easily. Anytime you experience an anxious feeling, simply take a deep breath and as you exhale say mentally the words "calm," "poised," "easy recall." You are calm and poised throughout the entire examination because you are calm and confident. You work with the highest efficiency and you do it easily. When the examination is over, you are confident that you have scored the grade that you want.

Your powers of observation and awareness are improving greatly with each passing day. All that you read, hear and feel is fully detected, integrated and stored in associated patterns in your memory. You possess the key to unlock the stored memory patterns, and whatever you wish to recall flows instantly into your conscious awareness. You know that your concentration and retention are constantly improving. Your quest for knowledge keeps you mentally alert and searching. Each day you are thrilled and delighted by the rich, abundant variety of ideas and exciting philosophies that come before you. The intensely creative part of you is enriched and strengthened with each new insight. Whenever you need to remember, you send an order to your subconscious mind, an order to deliver the full and correct memory, and the idea appears with perfect clarity and form. Each time you use your memory to its full capacity you feel a deep, satisfying, inner warmth that comes from pride in yourself and your continuing success. You feel great confidence in the phrasing and organization of your ideas. You are exact and to the point. This rich confidence in your skillful use of your learning powers causes your concentration to become better, more effective, more permanent with each passing day.

Your subconscious mind is a well-spring of abundant, creative information. It contains all of the answers that are needed, and it instantly responds when needed in a calm, clear and easy way. For you, learning is a pleasurable experience. Your desire to learn is a powerful driving force that constantly motivates you towards the realization of your full potential for intellectual growth. The full understanding of what you learn comes easily, completely, and in an organized way. As your stored knowledge increases, your confidence grows by leaps and bounds. You speak with assurance on subjects you have studied, knowing you can command your subconscious mind to send forth this knowledge whenever you want it.

Because of this awareness your whole being radiates an inner glow as you work or play, revealing you as a witty, informed and expressive personality. You concentrate with an intense single mindedness, much as a river flows from its source to its mouth. Like a river, your mind flows from its source to its mouth. Like a river, your mind flows in one direction seeking out ideas and answers to the problem. As your mind flows, it grows as a river grows, with many streams flowing into it. Becoming vibrant, always seeking, searching, probing. Whenever you focus your concentration, whether upon a worn textbook or the daily newspaper you are cheerfully energetic, relaxed and poised. Printed words cause you to integrate your experiences with the ideas presented. You understand ideas the first time you encounter them. You are now reading more material rapidly and easily. Images form clearly and precisely. The relationship of ideas and concepts become clear and open as you absorb new material. As you quickly read a text you automatically find the main ideas and you instantly create a mental outline. Because you are constantly aware of the purpose of your studies and because you hold the vision of your goal constantly before you, you have continual success in your learning experiences.

Your subconscious mind is a perfect memory core. It is the sum total of all that you have studied and all that you have experienced. You are thrilled and delighted by the meaning and significance of your easy access to your subconscious memory. You continually grow in your capacity to absorb and use good information. You filter out and reject whatever is not needed. People respond to you because of your extraordinary recall, retention, your scope of interest and your depth of knowledge. This pleasant experience constantly and continually repeats itself. You are thrilled to have such a sharp and well organized memory. Now each of these ideas are making a vivid, deep, permanent impression on your subconscious mind. Not just because I have spoken to you, but because of your intense desire to incorporate these ideas into your subconscious mind. You recognize the foundation of truth from which these ideas emerge. You are becoming free of any and all beliefs you may have held in the past about your capacity for using your mental powers. Each repetition of the ideas opens up new levels of awareness for you, stimulates new insights about your true potential for the creative use of your perfect memory.

Now I am going to count from one to five. At the count of five, let your eyelids open, and you are calm, rested, refreshed, relaxed, fully aware and feeling good in every way. One: slowly, calmly, easily, gently return to your full awareness once again. Two: each muscle and nerve in your body is loose and limp and relaxed and you feel wonderfully good. Three: from head to toe you're feeling perfect in every way, mentally perfect, emotionally calm and serene. Number four: your eyes begin to feel sparkling clear, just as though they were bathed in cold spring water. On the next number now, eyelids open and fully aware and feeling good. Number five: eyelids open, now take a deep breath and fill up your lungs and stretch.

*Richard J. Palmer, C.Ht., received his hands on training in 1987 at Rob Robinson's Institute for Hypnotherapy and his B.A. from the Institute for Hypnotherapy in Santa Anna, California. He is currently completing his doctoral degree and practices in a clinic in Fayettesville, Arkansas.*

# 46

# Inner Golf

## Guide: Doss Knighten, M.S.

*"Practicing successful images enhances performance."*

### Introduction

This journey has been useful to golfers and other persons doing athletic activities. It gives them focus and concentration necessary for optimum performance. In my work with athletes over the years, I found that many who succeed have the unique ability to visualize their performance prior to the action. This gives them a greater realization of their potential.

### The Journey

Close your eyes and when you are ready, imagine you are able to see a golf course, with green grass and trees lining the course in each of the fairways. Now imagine that you are playing the game of golf, and you want to focus your concentration in such a way that you have no distractions from the easy comfortable, powerful stroke that you hope to make — swinging the club and having the ball flying in the direction that you wish.

Now imagine your feet positioned firmly on the ground. You now grip the club firmly. The head of the club rests behind the golf ball. At this point you breathe very deeply. Look down the fairway and imagine a line that the ball will make through the air, much as a tracer would make coming out the end of a gun barrel. You can see the bright line that the ball will make as it flies through the air. Now as you look back to the ball, you focus all of your attention on the club and the ball. Hold your head steady as you begin the back swing. As you bring your back swing up to its highest point, cocking your wrist, you feel very, very relaxed. Watch the ball closely, and begin the down swing with your club, watching the ball. As the club head swings on its downward arch, your body moves into the stroke. Your hips and shoulders move through. You feel the club head strike the ball and your club swings up with the follow through. You have completed the swing, and you look down the fairway and see the ball landing in the distance right in line with the line you visualized.

Now let us start again. Repeat the same process. Position the ball, look down the fairway and create the line. Look back at the ball, begin your back swing. Cock your wrist. Now begin the down swing, striking the ball with the follow through. It becomes very easy for you to pay no attention to and lose awareness of anyone standing nearby. Your total focus is on striking the ball.

### Pause

Change the scene and move to the green. You now have your ball laying on the green. You take your putter in your hands. Position your feet firmly on the ground. Address the ball with your putter. As you look from the ball to the hole, you will again see a bright line. Look back at your putter again, take a deep breath, relax and begin your back swing, focusing on the ball. You start your down swing with a nice, easy, comfortable stroke and an easy follow through. The ball rolls down the line toward the hole and drops into the cup.

**Pause**

Again, imagine you have the ball sitting on the green and are to repeat the process. Observe the bright line from the ball to the hole. Position your feet firmly on the ground. Start your back swing. Allow yourself to strike the ball with a very easy stroke and watch the ball proceed towards the hole. Repeating this experience, practicing it, and visualizing it with each shot will allow you to have a greater and greater sense of control of your concentration and to minimize any distractions that might interfere.

*Doss Knighten, M.S., lives in Gladstone, Oregon, and is a licensed marriage and family therapist with twenty five years of experience. She is also a management consultant and organizational developer for government and private businesses, and she has been an athletic coach.*

# 47

# Turning Insight
# Into Action

## Guide: Martin L. Rossman, M.D.

*"Bringing your insight down to earth can
be called the process of grounding."*

## Introduction

Without "grounding" — your imagery work may remain
**mere** fantasy. In ground, you take the imaginary and make
**it real.** Choice has to do with will, and the act of grounding
**is an act** of will.

The following script will guide you, step by step through the
grounding process. It is different than other guided meditations in that it does not require you to enter a deeply relaxed
state until you reach the stage of mental rehearsal. Have
writing materials at hand, and take as much times as you
need to work through each stage. There is no predetermined
time period for this process. It could take you as little as thirty
minutes or as long as the rest of your life, depending on the
magnitude of the issues you are working with, the clarity of
your insight, and the presences or absence of resistance to
your change.

## The Journey

Take a comfortable position, and have writing materials at hand. During this exercise you will often have your eyes open and will be writing. There is no need to do deep relaxation until you reach the stage of mental rehearsal.

The process of grounding is something you may or may not do well instinctively. The following process breaks it down into steps that allow you to make change happen from your insights.

The first step is to *clarify your insight.* Take some time to state to yourself as clearly and simply as you can what you have learned that you wish to act on. Write down the clearest sentence you can that expresses that insight. Carefully look at the sentence you have written and decide which word is the most important one in that sentence. Look at each word carefully and make sure that it is just the right word to express exactly what you mean. Take as much time as you need to do this.

**Pause**

Next, *think about your insight* and list several possible ways you might practically act on that insight to make the changes you desire. Brainstorm this—take a large sheet of paper and write down as many ways as you can think of that would be a step in this direction. Do not edit as you write. List all possibilities that come to mind, whether realistic or not.

Look over your options—can you combine any? Which would be the most practical for you to actually carry out? Which would be the simplest? The easiest? Is there one way which promises the most success or the greatest return for the least effort?

When you are ready, *choose* the option that seems the most realistic and promising for you. Circle that choice on your list.

The next step is to *affirm* your choice... to put your energy and resolve behind it. It often helps to state your choice aloud. Repeat to yourself several times "I choose to... " whatever it is you have decided to do.... Make you affirmation aloud.

### Pause

The fifth step is to *make a concrete plan* for carrying out your choice. Consider what specific steps are involved and in what order.... Who might you have to speak to, and what might you have to do?... Make a specific plan in simple, yet detailed steps.... Write it down, making sure it is clear and practical.

### Pause

Now *rehearse your plan in your imagination*.... Close your eyes and take a couple of deep breaths... and invite your body to relax as it has so many times before. Just allow it to be at ease and comfortable where you are. As you breathe gently and easily, allow your mind to become quiet and still.... You may want to go to your quiet inner place and become comfortable there.... When you are ready, imagine yourself actually carrying out your plan.... Really use your imagination to see and feel yourself carrying out your plan from start to finish to give yourself a sense of what may happen in real life.... Notice which parts seem easy and which parts are harder.... During your imagery you may become aware of obstacles to carrying out your plan.... These may be events, people, or simply feelings and attitudes that arise as you begin to act on your plan.... If you do envision such obstacles, adjust your plan to account for them.... You may find you need to change your plan or break it down into smaller steps to make it happen.... Take all the time you need to adjust your plan until you can imagine yourself carrying it out successfully.

**Pause**

Repeat your imagery rehearsal, imagining yourself successfully carrying out your plan several times, until you feel comfortable with it.... This will help you energize and support this new way of acting and reacting for you.

When you are fully ready, open your eyes and become wide-awake.... Take some time to write about any changes or adjustments you've made in your plan... and about any obstacles you have anticipated and how you might deal with them if they arise.

The final step in grounding is to *act* on your plan. Carry it out in real life for a certain amount of time.... As you do this, continue to be observant of your thoughts and feelings and notice how others react to you as you act in this new way. Notice where you are successful and where you enjoy this new way... and also notice where you have difficulty, if you do.... Do any problems you didn't anticipate arise as you act on this plan?... If so, how might you adjust to account for them?... Life is a continuous process of adjustment and refinement... pay attention, and you can learn to make change happen in the easiest and most effective way.

# 48

# Skill Rehearsal/
# Master Teacher

## Guide: Maureen Murdock

*"Your master teacher can help you improve
any skill you wish."*

## Introduction

In this exercise, we use the image of a "Master Teacher" to
help improve a specific skill. Begin by choosing a skill that
you wish to improve or perfect. It may be soccer, writing,
painting, or whatever it is that you wish to improve.

The children who have used this imagery, have reported
invoking Pelé to improve soccer kicks, Haydn to tutor piano,
and Mark Twain to put some humor into their writing. They
also call on the help of friends, relatives, and mythological
characters.

## The Journey

Stand with your weight evenly balanced over your feet and
take a deep breath. In your mind's eye, see yourself involved
in the skill you have chosen to improve. Now practice it for
a minute with your physical body, as well as you can in the
space in which you are standing.

Now practice it for a minute with your kinesthetic body.

**Pause**

Now sit down in a comfortable position and close your eyes. Focus your attention on your breath, following your breath in... and out... of your nostrils. As you continue to breathe, you find yourself becoming more relaxed.

Now imagine that you are out hiking and you find yourself on a path in a very thick forest. The forest appears to be very friendly, so you continue down a path until you come to a group of very tall trees. As you approach this group of trees, you notice that one of the trees has a door in it. You open the door and walk into a small hallway. The hallway leads you down a stone staircase. You begin to go down the stairs, down... down... down. Finally you come to a great room that is filled with wonderful inventions that you have never seen before. You walk around the room, amazed by all that you see. You follow another corridor until you find yourself in a room that feels very peaceful and familiar. There you meet the Master Teacher of your skill, someone who can teach you all you want to know. This Teacher may speak to you in words or in actions; either will be very effective for you. You have three minutes of clock time equal to all of the time that you need to learn from your Master Teacher.

**Pause**

Now you will leave your Master Teacher, thanking this person and knowing that you can return any time you wish. Walk back through the corridor, through the room of the marvelous inventions, up the staircase, and out through the door in the tree. You close the door and walk back through the forest. And then you find yourself sitting here. When you are ready, open your eyes, stand up, and rehearse your skill with your physical body.

### Pause

Stop. Rehearse your skill with your kinesthetic body.

### Pause

Now again with your physical body.

### Pause

Now this time, as you do it again with your kinesthetic body, notice if there is more for you to learn about your skill. Is there a new approach that you can try? If so, try this with your kinesthetic body and then again physically. Notice any improvement that you have made, and notice too, how you feel about your ability.

*Maureen Murdock is an educator, therapist, and artist. She discovered the benefits of guided imagery with her own children and then took these techniques into her classroom and therapy practice. She has conducted workshops across the United States and Canada for therapists, teachers, and parents.*

From Spinning Inward: Using Guided Imagery with Children for Learning, Creativity and Relaxation *by Maureen Murdock Copyright © 1987 by Maureen Murdock. Reprinted by arrangement with Shambhala Publications, Inc., 300 Massachusetts Ave., Boston, MA 02115.*

Inner Child

# 49

# Inner Child

### Guide: Margot Escott, M.S.W.

*"Integrate your inner child with your adult self."*

## Introduction

This journey has been particularly freeing for adult children who are letting go of a painful past and beginning to heal relationships with parents. If you have suffered physical or sexual abuse, you may wish to work on this journey with a sponsor or therapist. Before beginning this journey, you might consider looking at some pictures of yourself as a child. You can enhance this process by drawing, spontaneously, right after you return from the journey. This is the time when your unconscious mind will bring up images and sensations through creative rather than verbal expressions. Playing gentle lullaby music such as Steve Halpern's "Lullabies" is helpful for this journey.

## The Journey

When you are in a comfortable, safe, relaxed position, begin focusing on your breath — in and out — like gentle waves coming in and going out. As you pay attention to your breath, let go of thoughts or feelings that you don't need right now. Allow yourself to drift into that pleasant state of trance where you feel comfortable and peaceful.

See yourself standing in front of an oval mirror. Reflected is a vision of yourself today. This is a special magic mirror. As you continue to gaze, you see that you are getting younger and younger. See yourself five years ago, then fifteen. See yourself getting smaller and smaller until you see an image of a very small child, perhaps three or four, five or six; whatever age feels right to you. This little child is smiling and extending his or her hand to you. As he steps out of the mirror you take hold of that small hand and begin to walk down a familiar road with that child. Feel the softness of that hand. Look at those vulnerable, trusting eyes. You may need to let that child know that you are a safe adult and are there to protect and play with that special child.

### Pause

You begin to realize that the familiar road on which you are walking is the street where you lived when you were very small. You and the child approach the front door of this dwelling, perhaps a house, apartment or trailer; and, if the child needs reassurance, you let him know that the worst is over and that he is safe with you. As you walk through the front door what do you see? What rooms are you in? Who is in there? What are they doing?

### Pause

You continue to walk through this place noticing the textures of the floors and walls. Noticing smells that are familiar from so long ago. You go into the kitchen. Who is in there and what are they doing? You walk to the family room and again note who is there and what they are doing. How do you feel? What does you inner child want you to know about this house and these people?

**Pause**

You now come into a very special room. It is the room of your precious inner child. He may have some things, special toys or objects, that he wants to share with you. Be aware of how full of life and wonder this child is. As you visit with the child, you let him know, that if he wants to, he may leave this house and come and stay with you. Let your child decide what he wants to do. If he chooses not to come today, tell him you will keep coming to visit him and he can leave with you whenever he wants. If your child decides to come, he may want to pack some things in a little bag or he may be ready to go right now. See yourself and the child walking back to the front door. As you start to leave the house, you see Mom and Dad standing in the doorway, waving and smiling good-bye. They seem happy to see you starting an exciting journey. You walk from the house, look over your shoulder and see them continuing to wave. You walk down that old familiar street and each time you turn around Mom and Dad are still there, getting smaller and smaller. You finally turn a corner, and they are no longer in sight. You find yourself in a beautiful place in nature and sit and hold that precious child in your arms. You may want to give that precious child some affirming messages like, "I am so glad that you are here; I will always love you; or You are enough." Be open to whatever that child has to tell you.

**Pause**

As you continue to hold the child, he becomes smaller and

smaller and smaller until he is so small that you could hold him in the palm of your hand. You gently place your magical inner child in your heart, and when you look down you see the eyes looking up at you and you realize that, from now on, wherever you are, wherever you go, you are carrying the precious cargo of that special child. Let yourself be giving to that child and attend to his needs. Let the spirit of that child enter into you as you behold the wonder of each new day and the blessing of each new relationship that comes into your life.

When you are ready, slowly bring yourself back to normal waking consciousness.

*Margot Escott, M.S.W. is a social worker in private practice in Naples, Florida, where she uses visualization and guided imagery for stress management, pain control, and recovery from addictive illnesses. In 1992 she received a national grant from The Humor Project for her work on the Humor Cart at Naples Community Hospital. She presents workshops throughout the United States on "Healing with Humor and Play," "Discovering Your Inner Child," and "Visualization for Success."*

# 50

# Journey into Childhood

Guide: Mina Sirovy, Ph.D.

*"Childhood dreams are simple and inspirational."*

## Introduction

Creating fantasies are easy when you let go of the adult programming and immerse yourself in the simple, spontaneous world of the child where life is flowing. This journey was created upon request shortly after I had just finished an afternoon meditation of getting in touch with my own inner child. I wanted to share my delightful experience, and I found that is was easy to sit down at the typewriter and record my reality as a fantasy! This experience also served as the beginning to my writing endeavors and opened up my creativity.

## The Journey

As you close your eyes, take a deep breath. Feel your body slow down. Your breathing deepens, your body settles in, the heart slows and your mind clears. Allow all thoughts to simply pass by without emotion or analysis.

You walk down stairs, one step at a time, relaxing more with each step. Let your feet sink deeply into the carpeting on the stairs as you count twenty steps, going deeper and deeper into relaxation. When you reach the bottom of the stairs you feel safe and relaxed.

**Pause**

Decide now to go outdoors. Walk to the door, turn a golden key and open it on to a beautiful outdoor scene. Ask yourself, as an eight-year-old, what would be fun to do on this beautiful day? What did I do at recess that I liked? In your mind's eye, walk down a grassy slope on your short eight-year-old legs and come to a lovely green park. Suddenly you have roller skates on your feet, and they propel you up and down and around on the concrete walks that swerve through the park. You are exhilarated and free!

**Pause**

You notice a swing set; so you remove your magic skates and sit on the swing. It's fun to see how high you can go on your own power. You pull back your legs on each back swing and launch out farther. Soon you're flying, looking up at the beautiful blue sky, the thin, pale crescent moon, and a few wispy clouds. The wind is blowing its mellow breath on your face, hair and cheeks, and you laugh for the freedom of it all. Yes, there's a silver slide that you must try. It winds down and is fun for one way, but too structured for your newfound free self. Just at your feet there is a discarded jump rope, so you pick it up gleefully, jump a few times, then sing and dance.

**Pause**

What a wonderful day you are having. No cares or responsibilities. There is a fountain of cool, refreshing water to soothe your throat. On impulse you stand under the high fountain and feel the water going down through your body as well as all over it. Feel it going down through your head, sinuses, throat and shoulders — relaxing as it goes, cleansing, healing, uncluttering. It's washing through your lungs, stomach, hips, thighs, knees, calves and ankles, coming out through your feet. Release all toxins in your system to the middle of the earth where they are purified in the center of molten lava. Feel the connection to the green earth. Step forward and feel the energy of the earth traveling up through your toes, ankles, legs, torso, neck and head. Feel the warmth of the energy, and see yourself inwardly and outwardly as a glowing being. Feel smaller than your body and more expanded than your body at the same time. You are a child and an adult all at once! You are not alone — you are all one. You are you and that's enough. You are here now, not a human doing but a human being.

Your body keeps breathing as you count slowly from one to ten, coming up, coming back, feeling refreshed and revived. And so it is.

*Dr. Mina Sirovy, who resides in Oceanside, California, is a marriage, child, family therapist with degrees in psychology from the University of California; a master's degree from United States International University; and a Ph.D. from The Professional School for Psychological Studies, where she was also a professor. Dr. Sirovy is a transpersonal psychotherapist who calls herself a "stretch" instead of a "shrink."*

# 51

# Mother

## Guide: Larry Moen

*"She represents the love you desire and cherish."*

**Introduction**

Your mother is the affectionate person who gave birth to you. She is your source. She represents the qualities of nurturing and love. In this imagery, you can become united with a figure that represents the Universal Mother in the cycle of birth and death. If your own mother was not nurturing you may choose to visualize a loving grandmother, the Divine Mother, or Mother Earth, as your Good Mother.

The ability to love is available to those who see no obstacles and who love unconditionally without judgment. We all have that ability, but many of us can not access it. Use this imagery to find the source of love and nurturing represented by your Good Mother. Use it to release from the confinement of prejudices that shape your emotions about your mother.

Begin your journey to the place of "Oneness" with your

mother because she is the symbol of the starting point —
the source and origin of your life.

## The Journey

Close your eyes. Let your mind relax and drift gently until
you find yourself standing at the top of three steps. Take
the first step down. Your muscles relax. Feeling heavier
with each step, descend to the next level. You come to the
third and final step. You step down and are totally relaxed.

You are any age you choose to be at this time. You begin to
walk forward. In the distance you see a house. As you approach, it becomes clear to you that this is your Good
Mother's house. This is where she lives. You come closer
and upon reaching the door you knock. Your mother opens
the door and is standing before you. You step forward and
embrace her. This hug unites you both. It represents total
acceptance from both of you. She accepts you and you accept her, unconditionally. During this visit you let down all
walls. You open yourself to her and let her in. You are free
to express yourself knowing it is safe. You love her with all
of your being, body, and spirit. You both walk through the
house to the kitchen. As she sits on a chair, you pull another directly in front of her. You sit down, facing her,
looking deeply into her eyes. Tell her something that you
have always wanted to say to her.

**Pause**

She is receptive to everything that you have told her. She is appreciative of your openness and your honesty, and she is proud of you. You will always be in her heart and soul. Words that you have feared for so long weren't so hard to say after all. You take her hands in your hands. You rise together, hold each other and walk back through the house to the front door. You hug each other, then the two of you separate, and you leave her standing at the door as you walk farther and farther away. You turn and wave. She waves back and the palms of your hands unite at a distance with a beam of energy and a oneness between the two of you. A oneness at a distance. The energy between your palms is strong, healthy, and mature. This is the woman who has given you birth. She is a tower of strength and you are a part of her. The two of you are united in a healthy way, healthier than ever before. You place your palm to your lips and blow her a kiss that she catches in her hands and holds against her breast. Knowing you can return at any time, you find yourself at the base of three steps.

As you step up to the first step you become more awake, more energetic. You feel your body again, light and relaxed. Step up to the second step, awakening with each step you take. Gently stretch and release every muscle in your body. Now step up to the third and final step. Take a deep breath, exhale and, when you are ready, open your eyes.

# 52

# Seeking Enlightenment

## Guide: James C. Knight, Jr.

*"In memory of my teacher, Cash Bateman."*

### Introduction

This journey was given to me in 1960 by my teacher, Cash Bateman. The results have been beneficial for many years and only recently have I been able to share this to benefit others. Whether practiced alone or in a group, this meditation helps release present apprehensions while energizing the physical body. Pine represents energy; golden water, spiritual energy; the pyramid, strength; the altar, releasing emotions; and the stars, setting goals. This meditation also helps to release fears, stress, and other emotional problems. It also gives one strength to bring forth a loving spiritual energy and the recognition that as you travel through this lifetime, you will have positive and negative days in the hills and valleys of life, but that by utilizing this technique, one is able to cope with all types of problems.

### The Journey

Close your eyes and visualize before you two rows of tall pine trees. Begin to feel their vibrations. Listen to the wind as it blows softly through the branches. The wind brings to you the fresh scent of pine.

Draw this scent into your being. Walk from east to west between the two rows of pine trees. As you come to the other end of the path, see a swimming pool twenty feet wide and thirty-three feet long. This pool is filled with shimmering water that has a golden glow. Standing at the edge of this pool, visualize bathing in this glow for a few moments.

**Pause**

Now remove your outer garments. Feel the wind and the glow. Now enter the pool from the east and swim or float, slowly letting the refreshing water surround your body. Immerse your entire body in the refreshing gold water. Feel it flow through you, softly, gently, going into your pores, deep within you. Enjoy the feeling. Feel the water flow over you as you move. Enjoy this feeling as you move.

**Pause**

You are now on the west side of the pool. Step slowly out of the comforting and cleansing water. Two guides are there with towels to dry you. They present you with a robe (color of your choosing) and place golden sandals on your feet. When they are finished, you look up, and see a pyramid.

At the entrance door say the words, "I am one with the Christ Spirit. May I enter?" Then proceed three quarters of the way up to the top. Visualize a room with an altar made of beautiful marble.

As you go to the altar to kneel. You see a window before you. Pick out a star in the heavens and say, "Guide me over the hills and valleys so that I may not stumble; let me lift my left hand up towards Thee as my right hand, I extend to help others." Remain in this position for a few moments and receive the enlightenment that comes from your guides.

## Pause

Slowly relax and come out of the meditation.

*James C. Knight, Jr. is a certified and licensed hypnotherapist in Fort Lauderdale, Florida. He is part-owner and president of several corporations including ISMBF Inc. and Delarosa Vine Industries Ltd., which distributes Grapeseed Oil in the western hemisphere.*

# Male/Female

# 53

# Aphrodite

### Guide: Mary Ellen Carne, Ph.D.

*"Appreciate the true meaning of feminine consciousness."*

## Introduction

This journey was created to counteract the negative imagery and messages that women often receive about their bodies in this patriarchal culture. It helps redefine, reenact, and empower a woman's concept of the beauty and sacredness of her body as a reflection of her Soul/Self. I use this guided imagery to bring wonder, appreciation, and true meaning of the feminine consciousness and body awareness.

## The Journey

Go to that quiet place, your center; focus on your breathing to get there. Let go, and when you are ready, feel yourself descending a spiral staircase that brings you to the place within, where you find your power. The best way to know the Goddess Aphrodite is to experience her within yourself.

### Pause

Descend your spiral stairs and when you reach the bottom, find yourself on a beach, a warm, beautiful sunlit beach.

Allow your eyes to look around and take in all that is there for you.... Now find your eyes looking out over the water, a beautiful, sparkly, clear, blue-green, ocean — a fathomless, ever-shifting sea, symbol of the essential female. Allow yourself to really "be" in this place of yours; take in its sights, sounds, smells and sensations. Take a moment to explore this special place of yours.

It is here in this splendid place that you will encounter Aphrodite. Aphrodite — golden one, primal mother of all creation, woman born of the foam of the sea.... Aphrodite — mediator between earth, sky and sea, our inner goddess who outwardly manifests herself to us as morning dew, the mist, or cloud, as fertilizing rain and as the sea.

Out on your ocean now, see Aphrodite carried along on the waves in the soft foam of the sea, accompanied by her sea nymph companions.... This is Aphrodite, virgin goddess in the original sense, one in herself, sensual but always independent, a blend of receptivity and focus. She is the intense love and understanding that connects, creates and begets all life. Have her move closer now. Aphrodite, a friendly, smiling, laughter-loving goddess who combines wild animal desire with the sophisticated arts of love. Her intelligence is intuitive, she harbors no anxieties or ambivalence about sex and her body, for she knows that she alone owns her body....

Let her now approach you and have her place a sparkling golden shawl around your shoulders and say to you, "Remember always that this goldenness of womanhood is eternally yours. You are Aphrodite, a part of me." You dance for a moment on that sunlit beach, celebrating this golden being that is woman, that is you.

## Pause

Once you have finished, Aphrodite approaches you once again and hands you a beautiful shell that she has brought with her from the sea. She lovingly gives it to you saying, "I give this as a symbol of your sexuality, that which belongs to no one but yourself. Rejoice in your power. No one but you may own or control your body. All acts of love of your choosing are my rituals. Let there be beauty and strength in your body, power and compassion, honor and humility, mirth and reverence felt in every cell of your being. Experience your sexuality as a force of transformation, not of possession or being possessed. Tap the Aphrodite energy that urges you to dance radiantly, to flow, soar and glow in joyful appreciation of your whole being...."

You are fully with Aphrodite now, alchemical goddess, the golden one, soul of the world, energy whose presence gives luster and brightness. Her energy shines forth from within, which like a magnet, draws waves of loving energy to you.... Aphrodite's love is a love far greater than just romantic or sexual love. She is also platonic love, self-love, deep friendship, soul connection, rapport and empathetic understanding. All are expressions of the love that Aphrodite draws to herself.

## Pause

And now it is time to view the ever-present "other side" of this wondrous alchemical force that is Aphrodite, for along with the strength of love comes strong passions of hate, rivalry, and jealousy as well.... Emotions that can provoke others to murder, to go to war, to feud with friends and relatives — Aphrodite's dark side. The love Aphrodite can arouse may sometimes turn to hate just as the consequences of love can sometimes be disastrous. Aphrodite's urge toward sweet desire, intense yearning, regardless of the end toward which it is directed, can lead to great suffering as well as joy, making her presence a sometimes frightening experience. While Aphrodite's energy is indispensable to life and creativity, if left uncontrolled, her power can also be all-consuming and destructive to our "selves." Yet Aphrodite *never* lets you forget that you *always* have choice and control in keeping a rein on her emotions.

### Pause

Lead yourself back now to your sunlit beach, rejoicing in your experience of *all* of Aphrodite. Sensing your wholeness, feel once again the warmth of the sun's rays, the ocean spray and the day's golden glow.... On your beach, in preparation for leaving her presence, create a sacred space in Aphrodite's honor, a place resplendent with symbols of her presence, the dolphin, the dove, the swan and sparrow, a golden apple, pearls from the sea, a beautiful shell, a lily, watermine, a rose or any other symbol that arises for you from your own inner place of Aphrodite.... Create a space of honor for her within you, a place to which you may return whenever you so choose.

### Pause

Aphrodite, the golden one, is the power, glory and magnetism of all forms of love. She embodies the aspect of the *feminine that of her own choosing* seeks relationship and union with "others." Find a way now to leave your beach and gradually return to the present bringing with you the memory of Aphrodite, flower goddess, she who whispers from the ocean, lover of laughter, giver of joy. Where she walks, the earth blooms beneath her feet and draws forth the hidden promise of life. Remember, she is always and forever a part of you.

# 54

# Male Development

### Guide: Loyd White, Ph.D.

*"Return to the symbolic life and experience the
internal nature of being a man."*

## Introduction

This journey was created for male development workshops.
It assists men in returning to their inner life, their symbolic
nature. It is helpful in balancing and integrating the task
driver — the externally oriented male. I have found that
many men are out of touch with themselves and have lost
the source of the imagination. Without a sense of self,
outward activities take men further away from their centers.
I have observed men who have been numbed and cut off
from the internal process begin to show some feeling. As they
begin to feel self reflective, they become more attuned to
anxiety and the unrealized internal defense mechanisms. As
a result they are to reduce compulsive and addictive self-
sabotaging behaviors.

Most of all men who have previously seen no relationship
between family of origin issues and their life scripts begin to
return to early life relationships with father and mother in a
symbolic and non-threatening manner. A man has a starting
place for his psychological and spiritual condition as he
encounters the images that unfold in this journey.

## The Journey

Close your eyes or see a focal point on the ceiling. Take three deep cleansing breaths and relax.

Get comfortable with both feet on the floor. Experience Mother Earth's energies coming up through your feet. Feel her energies coursing up through your legs and all the way to your heart — the center of your compassion. Extend your right hand and allow Father Sky to touch your fingers. Take the energy of Father Sky in your hand as if it is a ball of white energy. Now take the energy of Father Sky and gradually move this energy toward your heart. Take this ball of energy and place it in your heart. Experience the uniting of Mother Earth and Father Sky. In this uniting, you experience the coming together of all your ancestors.

### Pause

Now I'm going to count down from ten to zero and as I do you will become even more deeply relaxed. Ten... relaxing nine... relaxing even more eight... seven... six... relaxing five... four... three... deeper and deeper relaxed two... and one... and all the way relaxed. As you reach zero, going all the way down, you see a door marked "The Pass." You pass through the door and enter all the way into your imagination. You are on a journey.

In your journey you come to a meadow by a mountain... you take whatever equipment you need for your ascent up the mountain... prior to your ascent, you take a vessel out of your backpack and view it in detail.

You begin your climb. At first it is a rather easy climb. Midway you stop for a rest and observe how far you have come.

You continue your ascent until you reach a precipice where you are stuck... you can neither go up nor down... a wise man extends his hand down and assists you to the summit... standing on the summit you observe the world below and then allow the sun to penetrate you... the sun's rays pull you into its center....

You come back down to the mountain top and observe the earth below... you descend to the meadow by the mountain. You take the vessel out again and observe it inside and out for any changes....

Now, leave this journey behind you and begin to come back to this reality. As you do take this experience with you.

One... coming up, two... even further, three... by the time you reach the top you will feel wonderfully good in every way, four... and five... begin to be aware of your surroundings, six... your senses become alive and you hear the sounds around you, seven... feeling very peaceful and calm — yet very alert, we reach eight... and you take three deep easy cleansing breaths, nine... and ten... that brings you all the way back to the surface feeling peaceful, calm, yet very alert.

*Loyd White, Ph.D., lives in Tustin, California, where he has a corporate training program called Exploring Gender in the Work Place. The issue of authority led Dr. White to an examination of fatherhood and masculinity in society. He leads workshops and groups devoted to the development of natural masculine attributes. He has authored a series of workbooks on life and career for the minority communities and has just completed a book on career transition that will soon be published.*

Children's
Visualizations

# 55

# Test Taking

## Guide: Margaret Holland, Ph.D.

*"The key to successful use of imagery in your work*
*with young people is your own enthusiasm."*

### Introduction

The following imagery has been designed to help students
overcome test anxiety and to be mentally prepared to do
their best in a test taking situation. The imagery incorporates
strategies that highly effective test takers frequently use. To
be most effective, the imagery can be modified to fit a specific
test situation — SAT, GRE, etc. It should be repeated several
times before the test.

### The Journey

Imagine it's the day of your big test. You see yourself getting
up that morning and putting on your favorite clothes...
clothes that are comfortable and make you feel good. Notice
exactly what you are wearing. Choose something that you
feel good in... that helps you feel calm and comfortable and
confident. Now you are dressed.

You arrive at school, and you enter the room where the test
will be given. You stand in the doorway. Look around the

room and feel a wave of confidence, knowing that you are well-prepared and that you will do well today... that you will do your very best. Now you walk into the room and you sit down in your seat. You feel the seat beneath you. You feel your arm on the desk or table. You hear the sound of other students. You look at the familiar room. Look at the walls and feel comfortable and ready. You feel your body in that perfect state of calm excitement, of easy readiness, and you know that you are in the best possible frame of mind to do well today.

**Pause**

And now you see your teacher handing out the test. You have your paper, your pencil, and you see the teacher hand the test to the person near you, and then give you your copy. You feel it in your hand and put it down on the desk in front of you. And as you look at it, you know you will be able to answer it easily and well.

And now you begin with the first questions. Feel yourself reading them easily and answering confidently. And if you come to something you're not sure of, you simply mark it and skip it, and go on... knowing that somewhere on the test there will be a clue that will help you know how to answer that part. Know that you will have plenty of time to come back and do your very best. So now you are continuing to answer easily, finishing question after question, breathing smoothly, feeling confident. And when you have answered the very last question, you go back and fill in any that you haven't answered. And then perhaps you check over your paper, not changing anything much but simply checking to see how well you have done.

And now it's time to turn in your paper. You turn it in knowing that you have done your very best and knowing that you've done as well as you could have done. You feel confident, sure, and proud of how well you have done. You look at the paper and smile with satisfaction and pleasure. Notice the good feelings and remember the calm feelings... the calm excitement that enabled you to do your very best.

Now let that scene fade away, knowing that's how you will do on the day of the test. And when you are ready, wiggle your toes, stretch, and open your eyes, and smile.

*Margaret Holland, Ph.D., is a professor of education at the University of South Florida in Tampa and a yoga teacher. She has a Ph.D. in Interpersonal Communication. She has done research in the effects of stress on learning and has worked with college athletes to improve their performance through imagery rehearsal.*

# Grief

# 56

# Grieving

## Guide: Jule Scotti Post, M.S.

*"Letting go facilitates new life to grow in time."*

### Introduction

This journey uses the imagery of autumn to help clients grieve and let go. It also uses the process of breathing to facilitate emotional release. I have found that clients who are in physical or emotional pain have some unresolved grief that they need to work through. This may be grief from loss through death or divorce or from the loss of a job, a home, a vision or a dream, We also need to grieve the lack of those things we never had — our childhood needs that were never met or our longings for love, for peace, for joy that have never been fulfilled.

This journey is a gentle invitation to begin the grieving process. It is best practiced with a friend or therapist so that someone is available to help process the deep inner feelings it might provoke. The breath is used to deepen the experience and also to anchor the client. Be aware that you or the person with whom you are working may not be ready to release all the grief at one time — do as much as is appropriate and return to this journey at another time to continue the process.

## The Journey

With our breath, we take in life, energy and love. As we breathe out we let go, we release, we empty ourselves to allow the new life to flow into us. Breathe out deeply, from the lower part of your lungs, from your belly, from your deep center, empty yourself. And now slowly let the air flow in, the life force, filling you, your chest expanding gently as your lungs are slowly filled to capacity.

The out flowing and in flowing of our breath. The ebb and flow of the tides. The exchange of energy between the earth and the heavens. We live and move and have our being between the breathing in and breathing out of life.

Now in your mind's eye, see yourself in the woods on a beautiful day, late in the summer. See the trees covered in green, hear the birds singing and smell the fragrance of wild flowers. You have been filled by the rich harvest of summer fruit; the earth has given you renewed strength and support to nurture you on your journey. And now invite those you love to join you in the woods, surrounding you, holding you. You feel strong arms around you and you feel your feet firmly on the earth. Pause to take in the depth of love calling to you.

### Pause

Now allow the passing of time, the days, the weeks, the months as Earth moves from season to season. You feel a coolness in the breeze as it blows through the trees. The sun's light is gentler now, and the leaves are changing color — red, gold, orange, although some are still green. Smell the dampness of the fall. Hear the quiet forest. Now the birds have flown. Now your loved ones have gone away, and you are walking through the woods alone, feeling the loss of love, of days gone by, longing for what you had, longing more for what you never had. Be aware of whatever you need to grieve.

**Pause**

Now as you breathe out, allow the deep sadness in your heart to flow up and fill you. Be aware of this feeling in your body. Perhaps a tightness, a heaving in your chest, perhaps a burning in your throat, a wetness in your eyes, an aching in your head. Feel the deep pain in your heart. Breathe deeply into your heart. Breathe it out. Let it go, get it flowing, get it up to your eyes, let it pour in waves of tears or long deep sobbing — let your grief, your longing, your loss, your yearning, your cry from the depth express itself in its own way according to your own deep, inner wisdom. Continue to breathe in and breathe out.

**Pause**

See how the trees become more and more beautiful as their colors change, and they prepare to release their summer green for the stillness of winter. You also become more beautiful as you grieve, as you change, as you let go and become still. Go deep into your stillness for the seeds of new life are there awaiting you. Breathe in and breathe out, feel the inspiration that comes with letting go.

**Pause**

Look how the leaves fall from the trees. The branches let them go. The branches bare themselves to the cold wind. The leaves pile up to crunch under your feet. You can also let go of whatever needs to die in you to make way for new life.

Feel in your heart the new possibilities for life as you allow the old, the past, the gone, to leave, to die.

Feel within yourself the perfect balance of life coming into you and flowing out of you. Let your breath flow gently, peacefully, in rhythm and harmony.

Now gradually begin to bring yourself back, leaving behind whatever you are releasing. Bring back with you peacefulness, acceptance and relaxation. Gradually allow your eyes to open, see the room around you, hear any sounds in the room. Take a few moments to become fully awake and alert. Breathe. Breathe.

*Jule Scotti Post, M.S., is psychotherapist who uses biofeedback and deep relaxation in the treatment of stress and chronic pain in a medical clinic in Maryland. She has a masters degree in Counseling Psychology and has trained intensively in the use of guided imagery and music in therapy. She has worked in private practice as a psychotherapist for nine years and has practiced meditation for more than twenty years. Recently she has studied the principles of Chinese medicine and also brings this perspective to her treatment of pain.*

# 57

# Sailing Through Grief

## Guide: Christopher S. Rubel, Rel. D.

*"Experience forgiveness and renewed love."*

## Introduction

This journey comes out of a personal experience, while sailing, where I dreamed and dialogued with several people in my past with whom I had difficult and traumatic separations. There was a release during this time that will stay with me for the rest of my life. At least two people close to me and several patients of mine in therapy have been given this same kind of release from "sailing" through their grief.

The bird, the warbler, seems important in leading the traveler to the feelings in this experience. Picture that little bird and let that picture become vivid before moving on. Make this sailing venture truly your own as the words carry you along. It will somewhat chance each time you embark on this water journey. Aloha!

## The Journey

Allow yourself to breathe deeply and feel comfortable, putting aside the felt-demands of calls unreturned, paperwork not finished, and anything that might distract you. Find yourself at the helm of a sailboat. It is a beautiful afternoon. The sea is quite calm. There is just enough helm to be comfortable, and your sloop seemingly is steering herself on an easy course.

You are alone. The boat is moving easily. There's no need to touch the lines, as long as your wind remains westerly. You see dolphins off the port stern. They are gliding gently about the same speed as your boat. You are more peaceful than you've been in months and have a sense of what it means to "follow your bliss." A small flying fish emerges and skims the surface for a distance, and as it re-enters the water with a small splash, you become more relaxed and your breathing is deeper, all the way to the bottom of your lungs, breathing slowly, deeply. Your mind is cleared of everything back at the mainland. You have been quiet for several hours, not even hearing your own voice, not whistling, not singing, just listening to the rigging and the water spinning off the bow and the stern, mixing in with your wake.

Suddenly, appearing with no warning, a tiny, yellow, warbler, with a black crown around his head, alights on one of the lines, just about a foot from your right hand. You say, "Hello," and watch him. He cocks his head this way and that, seeming to study you. He is about as big as a tennis ball and appears to be breathing very hard. He says, "Hello." You're startled, but intrigued. He continues, "My name is Warren." You tell him your name. You sail for a few minutes. Then you ask him, "Warren, where did you come from?" He answers, "I have been flying for days, tossed around higher than I've ever been, nearly frozen, and I'm completely lost. I thought I was going to land in the ocean and drown. I found this boat just in time." He is out of breath and takes a few minutes to continue. You listen to his small voice carefully, amazed at how clearly he speaks.

He says, "There were many others, and I don't know what happened to them. We were all together when the storm took us up and tossed us for hours. I think I was even unconscious through my trip," he says. You empathize with him saying, "It must be frightening to experience what you have been through." Then, you say, "I'm glad you landed on my little sloop and are safe, now." He says, "I feel so relieved and safe being aboard your boat. I was so far from home." He becomes very quiet. His tiny, feathered body is balanced on the line as the boat gently moves this way and that beneath his feet. You think of times you have felt far from home. You tell Warren you are glad he is with you and is speaking to you on this beautiful day in the channel. "Thank you for coming," you say.

You watch Warren and lazily tend your boat. Warren is hungry, and you don't know what to do. He obviously hasn't rested, eaten, or had anything to drink for too long. He's been a victim of weather and turbulence. He is certainly an alien. You find some ways you are alike. About this time, there is a woman appearing, coming up the stairs into the cockpit from the cabin and she has some cereal and some water in small bowls. She places them next to the rail on the cabin top and Warren quickly hops over to have breakfast. You watch the two of them. She is just a few inches from him as he eats and watches her. Her face is radiant and placid, bewitching to you. There was no effort in her appearing topside, and the gifts for Warren seemed to have been part of her fingertips.

"Who are you?" you ask. She looks directly at you, with a soft, somehow wry smile. She says, "You wouldn't know. You've never taken the time it would take to know me." She turns back to Warren, and you watch the two of them, again, feeling tremendous curiosity. You think to yourself, 'Who is this woman and how would I have known her?'

### Pause

Again, you ask, "Who are you?" She again looks at you. Her look is one of almost teasing scorn. You come to realize she is challenging you to go inside yourself and find who she is. She has some kind of long-term agenda with you. She says, "It won't be easy for you, but you might get to know me, if you are willing to gradually give up your attachments and limitations and follow me. I am all you have ever lost and all you have always longed for. I am all you have rejected and all you have refused to feel. I am all you have been unable to love and all of those who have loved you and not been able to reach you. You will not know me, now, easily. But, you may, if you simply ask to do so and will follow me."

You are curious. You know the feelings may seem to sweep you away, but you are not afraid of her now. As you concentrate on these feelings, you know you are being led to an important, perhaps spiritual place by her. There is something haunting and profound about her. You begin to follow her, leaving the boat and entering the water. Although you slide beneath the surface, you are able to breathe. She moves gracefully ahead of you, leading you on in an unknown direction. Swimming as fast as you can you cannot keep up with her, and you lose her, completely in the blur of the water and kelp ahead of you and around you. You come to the surface and see your sailboat, sailing by itself and swim as hard as you can, but you can not catch up to the boat. You wonder if you can keep going, and your life seems suddenly in the balance, but more precious than ever. You know this is the end of your life as you have been living it. Everything you have left behind is in shreds, undone, incomplete, and nothing is prepared for your possible drowning. You swim as hard as you can, hoping for some chance to get back on board, feeling just a bit of a fool and as though you have been tricked by a fantasy. You are deeply challenged and swim with everything you have, somehow less desperate, somehow more excited. You feel your life is more important to you than it has ever seemed.

It is clear to you now, that all your priorities have been upside down. Your unlived life is very evident to you. You are aware of deeper feelings and an openness to yourself you have not had before, or at least, for a long time. In the water, ahead, you see the form of the spirit woman, swimming. In a muffled, haunting tone, her voice reaches out to you, through the water, "I love you. Do you hear me? I love you. You are just fine. Keep on swimming and listen to me. I love you."

You ask her, "Where are you?" She answers, "It doesn't matter. Just swim." You feel somehow lifted in the water, and there is a new strength coming to you, as you press on toward the boat, sailing on her own, not too far off. You draw closer to the boat and see a small, yellow ball of bird, riding on the cabin top. In the cockpit, there are several people, watching you. You draw closer. They seem glad to see you. The stern ladder is down and you grab hold of it and pull yourself up. In the cockpit are several people, who, at first, are not familiar to you. You look at them, letting your feelings come to focus and you realize you have not seen these people for a long, long time. You begin to recognize the faces and, as you do, you are able to feel a connection with each person in that sailboat cockpit.

Very slowly, now, one at a time, there are smiles of recognition. As you climb out of the water to the deck of the boat and step over the railing and into the cockpit of the sloop, one at time, the people there put arms around you. You feel the healing warmth of their arms. You are able to tell each person something you have needed to say. Then, you listen, and hear what each person has to say to you.

**Pause**

Look inside, at this moment, and detect elements of yourself coming together into new patterns. There is a growing sense of healing and restoration rising within you. Perhaps the people in that cockpit with you change, and you are able to be reunited, reconciled with others in your life at this moment. It is a mystical, spiritual, healing time for you. You realize it is for the others too. Let yourself stay in this setting for as long as you like.

**Pause**

Close ahead, off the bow, is a special island. It is a very peaceful place, and you are gliding in very calm waters toward that mooring at this moment. With the sails down and stowed, the boot glides effortlessly toward her mooring. Again, the inner voice comes, softly and confidently calling your name, several times, arousing your attention. The voice says, "I give you that peace which passes all human understanding." The voice becomes the voice of someone you love, perhaps someone you have missed or from whom you have felt estranged. The voice may change as it speaks, but you will recognize the speaker as the words become clear to you.

It is also clear the task is to return to this place often, to let these feelings of healing deepen. Your project in "walking the mystical path with practical feet" is to return to this place as often as you like, letting go of felt-demands, relaxing, taking the deep breaths, and letting go, returning to this sailboat, this mooring. As you breathe deeply and return slowly to a more alert, invigorated present place, feeling confident, feeling the strength returning to your body, there is another word from deep within you. You recognize the voice of the woman on the boat, as she says to you, "You are a child of the universe. You have a right to be centered, peaceful, healed, and free of all grief and pain. You have a gift of receiving this healing and living fully in the present, with more to give than ever before."

Enough! Let it deepen. Cherish this awareness. Let your heart receive this. Let consciousness absorb this healing, revitalizing journey. Each time you repeat this journey, you will be strengthened and enriched by the images, the feelings, the words, as you realize increasing peace of mind, courage, and desire to give and receive in closer relationships.

*Christopher S. Rubel, has a doctor of Religion in Pastoral Psychology from Claremont and an A.B. from Redlands University. He has been licensed as a psychotherapist since 1967 and practices in Claremont, California. He is also a priest in the Episcopal Church who likes to think of his endeavors as "soul work."*

# Past Lives

# 58

# Past Life Regression

## Guide: Chrystle Clae

*"Lifetime to lifetime, you remain
the same spark of Divine Light."*

## Introduction

There are many instances in our lives that feel unreasonably familiar. The idea that we have lived before is a possible explanation. Whether you remember a valid former lifetime or simply make up a story from your subconscious is unimportant. This journey may help you understand the reason for current relationships, talents, difficulties, and choices. I hope the experience of exploring another lifetime encourages your appreciation of just how special you are to those around you, yourself, and all life.

## The Journey

Take a seated, comfortable position, free of any disturbances. Begin to breathe deeply. In through your nose, hold to a mental count of five. Exhale slowly, through slightly parted lips. Repeat this process one more time. Continuing to breathe deeply, do some slow, very gentle neck rolls. Let your chin slowly fall to your chest until you feel the tension in the back of your neck. Take a deep breath into the tension and feel it relax and release. Bring your neck back up to center and let your right ear gently fall towards your right shoulder. Don't raise your shoulder to meet your ear. Just let it fall, until you feel the tension in the left side of your neck. Again, breathe into this tension and release it. Relax it.

Now, let your head slowly drop backward so that your chin seems to reach for the ceiling. You feel a slight tension in the front of your throat. Again, breathe into this tension; relax it, release it. Bring your head back to center and let your left ear fall gently and slowly towards your left shoulder until you feel the tension in the right side of your neck. Once more, you breathe very deeply into this tension and feel it instantly relax and release. Another deep breath, in through the nose and out, slowly, through slightly parted lips. Once more, and this time imagine that, as you inhale, the breath you inhale slowly is a soft, blue, powdery vibration that fills your lungs and your body with a feeling of the soft blue. Hold to another count of five. Exhale slowly and gently, through slightly parted lips, a soft pink vibration. A loving vibration that completely encircles you within and without.

### Pause

Now, sitting back with your palms up, feel the energy of the earth under your feet. It's warm and comforting. Let your feet feel like they almost melt into the earth. Feel very grounded, stable and certain of where you are. Tighten the feeling in the muscles in your feet. As you exhale, release those muscles and feel them soothed and free of tension. Now, tighten the muscles in your calf. Release it. Tighten the muscles in your thighs and buttocks. Now, release. Tighten the muscles in your stomach. Take a deep breath and release those muscles, relax them. You've massaged them and warmed them. Feel the muscles in your chest and your shoulders tighten. As you breathe deeply, you release and relax all the tensions and tightness you've been holding in your shoulders and chest. Now, make a fist with each hand and tighten it. Take a deep breath. As you exhale, release those fists and feel the tingly vibrations in your fingers which are relaxed and warm. Tighten the muscles in your face, around your eyes and jaw. Make them real tight. Take a deep breath and relax and release all those tensions that you've been holding in those muscles. Tighten the skull, the top of your head. With one more deep, deep breath, as you exhale, release your whole skull and top of your head. Feel your whole body completely comfortable and relaxed — relaxed, but feeling heavy, almost like there's a lead weight that is holding you still.

Continuing to breathe deeply, imagine that you are in a hall, a long hall. At the end of this hall, you can see that there is an elevator. Walk slowly towards this elevator. Realize that you are alone but feel very comfortable. As you approach the elevator, it opens. As the doors open, you enter this elevator. Once inside you see that it's brightly lit with color that's very comfortable for you. In this elevator there's a cozy chair for you to sit in. The doors close and you look above them to see, by the number that's lit, that you're on the eighth floor. As the eighth floor light goes off, the elevator begins to descend.

The lighting around you changes to a beautiful, soft lavender. Continue to watch the numbers above the door, as the number seven lights. Again, as the light goes off, know that it begins to descend and the light around you becomes blue. Sense how you feel as the lighting changes. Above the door you notice the number six light up. Again, the number goes off and you begin to descend once more. The lighting around you changes to a blue, a vibrant blue color. Once more, the number light shows and it's the number five. Continuing to breathe deeply you notice that the light goes out and, again, you begin to descend. This time the lighting changes to a soft yellow, and you realize the difference in how you feel in this yellow light vibration. You become more and more relaxed as you notice the number four light up above the door. You know as it goes out that you're descending once more. The lighting changes to an orange, a vibrant orange. An orange that gives you a sense of courage and ambition, anticipation for your journey. The number three lights up above the door. Again, the light goes off when you descend, lower and lower and more and more relaxed. The lighting around you becomes red. Now, above the door, you see the number two. Breathe deeply, more and more relaxed. The light goes out on the number, and the lighting around you gives up a beautiful, golden feel. All around you is gold. Realize how you feel with gold vibrations. As you descend, lower and lower and more and more relaxed, the light above the door shows you number one. As the car settles, the doors open.

Still breathing deeply, you look out from these open doors to a cold and dark room. Feel the emptiness in this room. Continuing to breathe deeply, feeling safe and relaxed, you now hold a candle. The candle is magically, instantly lit so that you can see further ahead in this room. It has a lower, sunken section. It's up ahead. It's where you're beginning to see a glimmer of light as you walk closer and closer. You see steps leading down to a warm and bright sunken fireplace. Blow out your candle. The light from the fireplace is fine. Slowly, walk on these worn stone stairs leading down to the fireplace. On the first step going down, you feel the warmth and the glow from the fireplace on your feet and ankles. Going down the second step, the warmth is felt in your calves and knees. Going down still, to the third, your thighs feel warm. Going down to the fourth, the trunk of your body, your stomach and your back are warm in the glow of this wonderful fireplace. As you go down to the fifth step, your shoulders are warmed. Down the final stair, the sixth step, your neck and your face, your whole body is basking in the glow of this warm, relaxing, crackling fireplace.

Listen to it crackling. Now, see that there is a beautiful, golden, circular ledge around this fireplace. Continuing to breathe deeply, you're comforted by this fire. You notice a soft cushion in your favorite color is waiting for you. As you sit, you gaze comfortably at the jumping, beautiful flames in front of you. You feel released from your shell of a body and understand the energy that is you, as you say to yourself "I am me. I am me. I am me." You gaze at the fire and a radiant light-being emerges from the fire to sit beside you.

You're thrilled as you see this light-being. You feel completely safe and at ease. This being telepathically tells you that it's your guide, your guide to your past. This being of light takes your hand and immediately you feel a sense of peace and light, of unconditional love. This being loves you just as you are. Truly you're protected, and you know it won't harm you in any way. Together you walk into the flame completely protected, completely immersed in cool, brilliant light. You are confident, safe and free. Your light guide tells you that you're approaching a period of time when you lived many, many years ago in another lifetime, a past life. Continuing to breathe deeply, very comfortable and completely relaxed, you sense that, with your guide beside you, you'll experience no anxiety or pain. No negative results that may have happened in this past lifetime will affect you now. You're simply an observer. And, remember, you're not alone.

Your guide touches your third eye area, the area between your eyebrows. You suddenly feel a surge of energy. This surge of energy sends your mind whirling. You're whirling and whirling. When the touch is removed you feel very grounded and realize you've traveled through time.

Instinctively, you look down at your feet. What do you see? What type of shoes? What size feet? Are you surprised? Can you tell what sex you are from your feet?

Now, look at the road that you're standing on. Is this road well traveled or is it hardly used? You now realize that you are walking into your home; the place that you live... the place that you lived in this past life. Look at the countryside around you. Do you recognize it as a place that you identify? How does it feel? What type of climate do you sense around you? Breathe it in.

Now, you see the place that you live in just ahead, off to your left. You know what country you're in. It's your country. Now, with another deep breath, quickly go to the door of your home and open it. Is anyone there to greet you? If there is, sense now what relationship they have to you. How are they dressed? Is there anything special that you feel from these people? If there's one special person there, look into his or her eyes. Know now if this person has come into your present life in another form. What relationship do you have with this person in your present life? Why have you come together? To work out a lesson that needs to be learned? To finish a goal together? Know, as you look into his or her eyes, why you may have come together again. Now, look around the dwelling. Notice anything on the walls? Any decorations, anything that comes to your awareness? Look at the floor. What is that like? Is there any distinctive smell in this place? What kind of lighting is there?

### Pause

The evening meal is being prepared, and you've been told to come sit down. You go to eat it. If there are others there, they join you. If you're sitting at a table what position do you take? Can you tell how old you are? Now, look around the table, and if there are others, view these others with the understanding of why you are together. Take your time.

### Pause

Look at your meal. What is this that's before you to eat? Who prepared this meal? Was it prepared in love? Is there anyone at this dinner scene that you sense has come again with you in your present life experience? Look into their eyes. Understand why you were together in this past life experience and why you've come together in your present life.

### Pause

Now, get a strong feeling, a sense of the most important lesson you had to learn in this lifetime of long ago. What was your purpose or goal for this lifetime? Is it a lesson that you completed, or is it one that you've brought with you in this lifetime? Instantly feel these answers.

### Pause

Is there anything in this past time that would relieve you or help you understand a problem in this current lifetime? Realize this now.

## Pause

Continuing to relax, and breathing deeply, you're comfortable and at ease and so thankful for this information. Your light guide once again appears to you, right beside you, and again, touches that special spot between your eyebrows. You once again whirl. Your mind whirls and whirls until you find yourself in another lifetime, a lifetime where you were filled with love. In this lifetime you knew you were joined with your soul mate. Look, as this person approaches. Notice the outstretched arms, the total feeling of love and acceptance. Look into these loving eyes and feel the completeness. The feeling of being loved just as you are. Just for the you that's inside. Let this beloved one embrace you. Feel your unity, your oneness — the overwhelming sense of love. Now, looking once more into this person's eyes, do you recognize this person in your present life? It may be a totally different relationship, but you'll get the same feel from these eyes.

## Pause

If you've come together again in this current lifetime, know now what you need to accomplish with this person. Don't think about it, just observe your first impression.

## Pause

As I count backwards from five to one, your guide removes it's touch. Five, four, three, two, one. You're once more alone, walking back to your comfortable spot in your current home. Again, as I count backwards from five to one, slowly awaken, remembering everything you've experienced today. Five, breathing deeply. Four, slowly awakening refreshed. Three, beginning to wiggle your toes. Two, wiggling your fingers. One, feeling completely refreshed, slowly open your eyes at a pace that's comfortable for you. Be filled with love and light and peace.

Now is the time to write down any experiences. Any insight or understandings into current relationships or current life purpose. From this day on, your life is enriched, beautifully enhanced with the feeling of unconditional love. A feeling that vibrates to all living things from the you, the inner you, with no judgement, no pain, nothing but love, light and peace to go forward with your life's work. May you have a life filled with light, peace and unconditional love.

*Chrystle Clae is an astrologer, psychic counselor, and teacher in Seminole, Florida. She is a nationally-known writer on the subject of metaphysics and she has a column for psychic advice in the* Suncoast Beach Reporter. *She is listed in* Who's Who in Service to the Earth.

# Global Unity

# 59

# Healthy World

## Guide: Louise L. Hay

*"Send some loving, healing energy to the planet every day."*

## Introduction

The planet is very much in a period of change and transformation. We are going from an old order to a new order, and some people say it began with the Aquarian Age — at least the astrologers like to describe it that way.... We are beginning to see our earth as a whole living breathing organism, an entity, a being unto itself. It breathes. It has a heartbeat. It takes care of children. It provides everything here that we could possibly need. It's totally balanced. If you spend a day in the forest or somewhere in nature, you can see how all the systems on the planet work perfectly. It's set up to live out its existence in absolute, perfect equilibrium and harmony.

## The Journey

Envision the world as a great place to live in. See all the sick being made well and the homeless being cared for. See dis-ease become a thing of the past, and all the hospitals now apartment buildings. See prison inmates being taught how to love themselves and being released as responsible citizens. See churches remove sin and guilt from their teachings. See governments really taking care of people.

Go outside and feel the clean rain falling. As the rain stops, see a beautiful rainbow appear. Notice the sun shining, and the air clean and clear. Smell its freshness. See the water glisten and sparkle in our rivers, streams, and lakes. And notice the lush vegetation. Forests filled with trees. Flowers, fruits, and vegetables abundant and available everywhere. See people being healed of dis-ease, so that illness becomes a memory.

Go to other countries and see peace and plenty for all. See harmony between all people as we lay down our guns. Judgment, criticism, and prejudice become archaic and fade away. See borders crumbling and separateness disappearing. See all of us becoming one. See our Mother Earth, the planet, healed and whole.

You are creating this new world now, just by using your mind to envision a new world. You are powerful. You are important, and you do count. Live your vision. Go out and do what you can to make this vision come true. God bless us all. And so it is.

*Louise L. Hay, a metaphysical teacher and bestselling author of nine books including* You Can Heal Your Life, *has assisted thousands of people in discovering and using the full potential of their own creative powers for personal growth and self-healing.*

*From* The Power is Within You *by Louise L. Hay. © 1991 by Hay House, Inc. Carson, CA. Used by permission.*

# 60

# Peace, Love & Joy

## Guide: Barbara H. Pomar

*"Love the earth; love the Self."*

### Introduction

This guided imagery exercise is helpful for restoring balance in the world and in receiving the love as it is returned and magnified many times.

It has been used to focus loving energy on "hot spots" in the world. Most participants have reported a heightened awareness of a *oneness* of immense magnitude as they emerge from this experience.

### The Journey

Loosen any tight clothing and find a comfortable position. Relax... Take a deep breath, letting your stomach stick out. Exhale the tension.

Starting at the feet, tense and relax each body part. Feet... tense and relax. Calves... tense and relax. Thighs... tense and relax. Buttocks... tense and relax. Hands... tense and relax. Abdomen... tense and relax. Chest... tense and relax. Shoulders... tense and relax. Neck... tense and relax. Roll your head gently side to side, forward and backward, around in a circle. Tense and relax your head. Take a deep breath and feel the brain and all the muscles in the brain and head relax.

Imagine a shaft of sunlight shining down on you. Feel its gentle warmth all around you. Imagine the light is a protective shield, allowing only love, light, and goodness in and reflecting anything negative or hurtful.

Now, inhale the white light down the spine, way down. Exhale... expanding the white light out. Be aware of the various energies around you: sounds... smells... lights... colors.... Identify each. Acknowledge each. Give thanks for each.

Now, inhale the white light down the spine, way down. Exhale up the spine through all the energy centers, which some people call chakras. As you exhale, imagine various colors flashing... red, orange, yellow, green, blue, indigo (navy blue), and purple. See them form a perfect ball of white light over the top of your head.

Expand that ball of light around you. Inhale the light. Exhale through your heart with love. This light, your personal energy field, is your love that you communicate with other beings.

Project the light in front of you (in the center of a circle). Feel the light grow and expand. As it expands, feel it start turning and spinning. Feel it continue to grow as you send love and light into the center of the spinning ball of light.

Feel it grow... imagine it... see it grow.... filling all around the circle with love and light, leaving peace and joy. All that it touches is filled to capacity with love, light, peace, and joy. It is too much for the circle, so it expands to fill the house, the neighborhood, the town (city or village). It fills the community, the county to the north, west, south and east. It leaves love, light, peace, and joy. The more it touches... the more it grows.

**Pause**

It expands even more. Further north, west, south and east.... It keeps moving in a spiral around the Earth touching every part of your country... leaving love, light, peace, and joy. The more it touches, the more it grows. Stop wherever you wish to center on troubled spots....

**Pause**

It expands even more... leaving love, light, peace, and joy. The more it touches, the more it grows. Stop wherever you wish to center on troubled spots.

**Pause**

It expands even more, traveling to the other side of the earth.... leaving love, light, peace, and joy. The more it touches, the more it grows. Stop wherever you wish to center on troubled spots.

**Pause**

It expands until it covers the entire planet. Imagine the entire planet Earth shining, flowing in love and light and filled with peace and joy. It is so filled with love and light and peace and joy that some of it is radiated into the solar system... into the galaxy... into the universe.

As it radiates out it is reflected back. Feel it as it is reflected back into your heart, mind, and soul... your entire being. As your entire being is filled with love and light and peace and joy. Spend a few minutes absorbing the love, light, peace and joy as it is being returned to you.

**Pause**

Now send the love, light, peace, and joy to those who you feel might need it... realizing that what you send, returns.

**Pause**

Take a deep breath. As you exhale, open your eyes and slowly move as you become more and more aware and alert.

*Barbara H. Pomar is a Certified Hypnotherapist (American Council of Hypnotist Examiners) in Salisbury, Maryland, specializing in hypnotic and non-hypnotic regressions (past, present, and future.) She leads seminars and workshops nationwide in meditation, past-lives, and dreams.*

# More Great Books

❏ *Meditations for Awakening*         $11.95
   Larry Moen
   ISBN 1-880698-77-3

❏ *Meditations for Healing*         $11.95
   Larry Moen
   ISBN 1-880698-69-2

❏ *Brain States*         $11.95
   Tom Kenyon
   ISBN 1-880698-04-8

# A Helpful Cassette

❏ *Creative Imaging*         $ 20.00
   Tom Kenyon, ABR
   Brain stimulation to increase visualization ability

Shipping         $3.00

         TOTAL_____

*Make checks payable and return with order form to*:
United States Publishing
Box 504 • Captain Cook • Hawaii • 96704

---

## ORDER FORM

NAME _____

ADDRESS _____

CITY _____

STATE / ZIP _____

PHONE _____